Deeply theological and pastorally sensitive, this collection of sermons opens the reader to the heart of one who continues to seek after the truth of God. Forthright and searching, Russ Dean encourages us to "put away childish things" in our belief system that we might journey further into the mystery of finding our lives bound up with the graceful cadence of the Triune God. This is the kind of disciplined thinking that can attract others to an examined and therefore richer faith.

Molly T. Marshall, Ph.D.
President and Professor of Theology and Spiritual Formation (Retired)
Central Baptist Theological Seminary

In this perceptive memoir, Russ Dean details his personal, spiritual and intellectual pilgrimage inside, outside, and alongside Christian community and concepts, much of it exemplified in his own sermons included throughout the book. Dean's journey of spiritual formation becomes an insightful guide for the rest of us.

Bill J. Leonard, Professor of Baptist Studies Emeritus
Wake Forest University

Russ Dean has written a book for all of us who feel like we lost our church home —like it slipped away from us, or was taken away from us, or just stopped feeling like home. Without a single trace of cynicism, Russ re-envisions Scripture, faith tradition and faith affirmations, hymnody and theology, finding in them truth, relevance, beauty, energy, and joy anew in a way that makes reading his book feel like we might find our way back home too. In these careful reflections on his own life, we are invited to consider this book as a treasure map that issues us our own invitation into a quest for a faith we can live with and into.

John Ballenger
Woodbrook Baptist Church, Baltimore, MD

In many ways, Russ Dean's memoir is an answer to the question: 'How did a nice, conservative kid like you become such an outspoken liberal?' But Russ answers the question as if he had asked it himself, digging down through the strata of his life like an archaeologist, uncovering one brilliant turning point after another and interspersing them with sermons that reveal the way his mind was changing and questions that invite us to change our own. Finding a New Way Home is a fascinating history of personal transformation, and I like the Russ Dean who emerges even more than the nice, conservative kid he used to be.

Jim Somerville
First Baptist Church, Richmond, VA

This fine collection of sermons by Russ Dean, Pastor of Park Road Baptist Church in Charlotte, is a model for other contemporary pastors struggling to proclaim a challenging and faithful Word from the pulpit. The sermons reflect the hard work of careful scholarship and demonstrate Dean's courage in allowing the biblical tradition to speak in honest and often creative ways. Remarkably, he is also committed to keeping abreast of current events and literature and to recovering (or perhaps even discovering for the first time) insights from his college and seminary studies. Dean understands the power of language in the pulpit and fully embraces his multiple roles as priest, sage, and prophet. A great resource for pastors and laypersons wrestling with faith and proclamation in these uncertain times.

John C. Shelley
Professor of Religion, Emeritus
Furman University

I find people, pastors especially, who embrace faith without struggle to be highly suspect. With raw honesty, Russ Dean invites us into his own experience, a window into "working out faith with fear and trembling." Grappling with essential questions about how God works in our lives and in the world, Russ Dean shows us how to embrace the questions and deepen our faith as we do.

Amy Butler
former Senior Minister, The Riverside Church in the City of New York

FINDING A NEW WAY HOME

The Unlikely Path of a Reluctant Baptist Renegade

RUSS DEAN

© 2020
Published in the United States by Nurturing Faith, Macon, GA.
Nurturing Faith is a book imprint of Good Faith Media (goodfaithmedia.org).
Library of Congress Cataloging-in-Publication Data is available.

ISBN 978-1-63528-078-4

Table of Contents

Suggested Reading

Diana Butler Bass, *Christianity After Religion*
Diana Butler Bass, *Christianity for the Rest of Us*
Rob Bell, *Love Wins*
Marcus Borg, *Meeting Jesus Again for the First Time*
R. Kirby Godsey, *When We Talk about God…Let's Be Honest*
Peter Gomes, *The Good Book*
Philip Gulley, *If the Church Were Christian*
Tony Jones, *The New Christians*
Anne Lamott, *Traveling Mercies*
Robin Meyers, *Saving Jesus from the Church*
Brian McLaren, *A New Kind of Christian*
Kathleen Norris, *Dakota*
Richard Rohr, *Falling Upward*

Foreword

This book is a memoir of my journey in faith. That journey began in the home of my childhood, but the chapters cover experiences extending from some of my earliest memories until just a few years ago. I had already begun reflecting on these experiences, theologically, as the later ones were occurring, but it was not until a friend invited me to speak to his congregation that I connected them. "You're not what most of our people think of when they hear the word Baptist," the priest of a local Episcopal church said. "Come talk to us about how you got where you are from where you started."

It was a fascinating challenge. As I sat down to prepare a one-hour Sunday school lesson for Episcopalian adults, I realized I had a story to tell. My suspicion is that this story, regardless of how eloquently I have or have not told it, will resonate with many people. Too frequently I hear people speak of their "bad experiences" with the church, experiences often occurring in the formative years of childhood or adolescence. Sadly, too many of these folks leave organized religion, if not turn their backs altogether on a God they suspect has turned a blind eye or a judgmental whim against them.

I have managed to stay within the realm of organized religion. In fact, it is my life. I have not felt the need to abandon or reject God. In fact, God has become more important, more real, more central to my story. I understand those who leave, but because I believe so strongly in the church and the value of faith in one's life, I hope my experience might be an encouragement. One can question, doubt, reject much of what we learned in our childhood, and still remain faithful.

There is a "new way home." Maybe my experiences will help some of you find it.

Each chapter includes a sermon I have preached over the course of the last eighteen years as co-pastor of the Park Road Baptist Church in Charlotte, North Carolina, with my wife, Amy Jacks Dean. I include these sermons as a testimony to the faith that has been developing and changing. I have enjoyed the privilege of being a "professional proclaimer" of Christianity, and although I did not write the sermons for this book, it should be clear in reading them that the faith which is very real to me continues to be a "work in progress."

Each chapter also begins with several "Questions to Consider." Unlike many books that conclude chapters with similar reflection/study questions,

I have included these questions as a prelude to each chapter. I hope they will whet your appetite and get your wheels turning in the right direction for the chapter and sermon that follow.

To get the most out of these questions, you might reflect on them briefly before you read and then come back to them before starting the next chapter. There is room for you to make notes about your own experience and any deepened insight you may have gained by reading my story and relating it to your own faith experience.

Finding a New Way Home is not just a book; it really is the experience of my life. I am glad to have this opportunity to share it with you. Especially if you have strayed from the path and have considered leaving it all behind, I welcome you. It's a journey worth taking, because even if you are surprised where you find yourself along the way today, you can be sure that home is where your heart is—and where God is—and there's just no place like it.

Welcome to the journey. Welcome home!

Note: As a means of emphasizing scripture, it has been our consistent practice for nineteen years as the pastors of Park Road Baptist Church to italicize all quotations of scripture. I have maintained that practice in this book, and all biblical quotes are from the New Revised Standard Version unless otherwise noted.

Where It All Began:
"Into My Heart"

Questions to Consider

Where did you first learn about faith? Who was your earliest teacher?

What emotions do you associate with those earliest memories of faith? Joy? Fear? Excitement, Boredom?

What is at the core of faith for you? Doctrines? People? Ethical convictions? The Bible? Fear? A way to get to heaven? Some mysterious, unspeakable experience?

Is there a difference between religion and faith for you?

Have your beliefs changed since your childhood? If so, how and why have they changed?

What is the difference in "faith of the head" and "faith of the heart"? Where did your faith begin?

Who is Jesus for you?

Do you think of Jesus as more like you or unlike you? How does your answer affect your ability to follow his example?

If your understanding of Jesus has changed, has that changed your understanding of God? How has it impacted your faith? Your ethical convictions?

❖

"We shall not cease from exploration, and the end of all our exploring
will be to arrive where we started and know the place for the first time."
—T. S. Eliot[1]

Sometimes people say to me, "I didn't understand all of your sermon today. You lost me at…." The way people say this makes me respond reflexively, at least outwardly, "Oh, I'm so sorry," but the truth is, internally, I'm not so sure. Should you actually "get it" all every time? What would that say of my preaching? And what of your listening!? Maybe it would say I'm the perfect communicator, which is doubtful. But it might mean there's not much challenge in the message, which I hope is never the case. It also may mean you're not actually listening close enough to hear the challenge!

So I'm not quite sure I understand the real problem. In all seriousness, when I hear this comment, I wish I had the courage to ask, "Did you get *anything* from the sermon?" And if you did not, let me ask, "Did you hear the choir? Weren't they great?" Or, "Did you hear the way Amy spoke the pastoral prayer?" Or, "In our moment of silence, did you 'hear' something then, feel something, get something from that *still small voice* (1 Kgs 19:12)? And what about walking in and walking out with friends along the corridor? Or did you sit near enough to someone that you felt the community of corporate worship, the fellowship of Christian community? Did any of *that* do anything for any part of you?

My point is that spiritual development doesn't come all together in some neat package at some precise moment. Could any of us ever really say, "Oh, yeah, *now* I get it!"

I'm not sure if I've ever gotten all of a sermon. Maybe it's just my slightly attention-deficit-disordered brain, my easily distracted, always wandering spirit, my no-moss-grows-on-a-rolling-stone soul, but when I'm listening to a sermon, or the radio, or the symphony, or the evening news, something generally pricks my attention—some word within all the words—and I'm off to the races. That word sends me into the clouds of my mind or down the spiritual rabbit hole of some journey of associations and affirmations and arguments. Maybe it's a hindrance to my learning, a deficit I need to overcome, but I've mostly accepted this way I process input as the way I process input (Is it really attention deficit disorder, or is the disorder being so attentive as to be overwhelmed in any given moment?). Whatever my disorder, I have learned it is who I am, and I have come to treasure the nuggets of meaning I get when I listen. Maybe it's just my small brain, but a nugget at a time is about all I can manage!

Maybe it's not just me. If we really believe in Truth—and all that believing in it implies—how much of a glimpse of Truth could we really handle at any one time anyway? When I listen to my amazing wife in her wonderful preaching (*listening* to sermons is a gift most preachers don't get to enjoy!), what I mostly come away with isn't the whole load, a complete outline of her message, a mental recall of her play-by-play delivery, all the nuances and allusions she poured into her stories. No, if I haven't been distracted by mentally forming the prayer I will offer when she's finished, or by the agenda of the administration committee meeting that will follow worship, or by thinking about getting the boat loaded and ready for vacation that afternoon; if I can pay attention enough that morning to come away with anything I can really hold on to at all, I'm grateful for it—one word at a time! If there's a single word, a turn of phrase, an image, an emotional stick, a spiritual "aha" that had sent my soul stirring before she said, "May it be so"[2] (inviting me out of my mind and back into the worship service), I consider it at least a good sermon and a great morning, indeed. And when she misses me altogether (or I miss her), there's usually a reason. Maybe I was still in the last verse of that last hymn, turning over the imagery in my mind, or I was still reveling in the lovely harmony of the anthem, or the sound that spoke to me in the silence was still deafening me to all the other noise in our order of service. When I miss it, I don't automatically assume it's her fault—though she *will* miss me sometimes; or miss "it," because preaching is art, not science, and human minds and spirits are unique and discrete (even when they are married souls!), and what speaks to one doesn't always touch another. So be it.

This book is not about preaching, but it is about sermons, or maybe I should say it is about "sermons." This book is about nine "words" that have been spoken along the course of my now-fifty-four-year life, through which I heard a voice, felt a touch, accepted a challenge, glimpsed a vision, was tantalized by Truth (just a hint of it!). As I stand just beyond midlife in this experience that I gladly affirm as a journey of faith, as I stand and look back, I can see that these words, insignificant nuggets at the time they were spoken, have guided my life. No one spoke any of these words with the thought of capturing all that is significant in one sentence or less. They were all spoken in passing, as offhand comments, or as a small part within a larger message. None of these statements was intended as a declaration of theological profundity: "Hear ye, hear ye…the following words will change your life."

But change my life they have.

I began this journey at an early age. Something about the religious life and experience spoke to me as a young child, and I have always been attentive—maybe a little obsessive at times! Maybe I was raised into it, tuned to a preoccupation with seeing and hearing some "calling" in life, or maybe there actually is a deep Voice running beneath and within all things, and maybe it's not possible to know the difference. What I know is that my life has been a journey, guided by serendipity and by chance, which may just be how God works in our random world, but as I look back, all those discrete, unintended "sermons" seem purposeful. As a discipline of awareness, an exercise of paying attention, this book is a reflection of that journey and those "mileposts" along my way.

The irony of those insightful "sermons," those mileposts of my journey, is that in one sense they have led me down a winding path that has taken me far from my home, miles from the safety and convenience and under-standability of the faith of my childhood (my childish faith?). The God in whom *I live and move and have my being* (Acts 17:28) looks nothing like the paternalistic and protecting and terrifying supernatural Father I read about in Sunday school. The Jesus who is the center of my ethical and devotional and theological conviction has come down from his lofty, untouchable divin-ity to embrace a unique but human incarnation. The Spirit, who completed the simple three-ness of my pious childhood deity, now pulses with universal and ubiquitous vibrancy, more akin to my very elementary understanding of quantum connectedness than a Holy Ghost revival.

An Oldsmobile commercial from years gone by tried to rejuvenate the image of a professional, if not stuffy, sedan by exclaiming, "This is not your father's Oldsmobile." I can think of no better metaphor for the ministry Amy and I have enjoyed and enjoined: This is not my father's Baptist church! The church my father served for twenty-six years as pastor was my home. That First Baptist community was filled with loving, committed people who served as models for an impressionable and eager young disciple, programs that engaged my boundless energy, and sermons and lessons that gave my faith content and structure. Children could do a lot worse than to be raised in such an environ-ment! But so much is different about the church Amy and I inherited. The setting is more urban and pluralistic, the people more worldly and diverse; the expectations for our leadership nudge us toward the prophetic edge of our pastoral vocation. In geography those two steeples are separated by two hours of interstate driving, and the churches marked by those "fingers pointing to God" are at least as far apart in theology and practice.

Miles from home suggests no arrogant superiority, but with honest objec-tivity I have to recognize that I am now a long way from where my faith began. I never intended this. I didn't set out to be a traveler, a wandering spirit. I have no rabble-rousing instincts. I've just followed. The mileposts I recall in this book trace that unexpected journey and the unanticipated joy.

Ironically, even as I acknowledge the distance I have traveled and admit that this path has been challenging, discomforting, even frightening at times, there is a strange sense that it is specifically in this "foreign land" that I now find myself back where I started. Like the ancient Israelites, exiled to foreign Babylon, I have not only made peace with this newfound faith, but have come to believe that only in *seeking the welfare of the* [foreign] *city have I found my own welfare* (Jer 29:7).

So this book is a narrative of "finding my way home" by the most unexpected of journeys.

A university degree did for me what education is supposed to do: It opened my eyes, broadened my horizons, expanded my faith—but not without stirring the pot first. Maybe that's also what education is supposed to do. Maybe without disturbing the equilibrium, nothing really changes. When introduction to philosophy, spring term of my freshman year at Furman University, challenged the comforting faith of my Baptist Sunday school experience, it was the first time I had ever known the tilting, off-centeredness of doubting. It was a little like walking through an earthquake. The ground seemed to be moving under my feet. I was frightened and angry, and Will Campbell was right when he spoke right to me during a chapel convocation toward the end of that freshman semester: "Once you get educated, nothing is ever easy again."

From that 1983 spring term, faith has always been more work than ease, more question than answer, more "a road to walk than a place to stand,"[3] and I have come to believe that is as it should be. From that moment of initial crisis, nine "sermons" nudged me along the way, at once "comforting the afflicted and afflicting the comfortable."[4] In the chapters that follow I will expand on those nine opportunities that presented themselves for my growth and the sometimes uncomfortable newness that expanded my faith each time. In the final chapter I will share how this winding road has led me back to the *faith once delivered* (Jude 1:3). It is the same basic faith with which I began, though an experience to which I have returned—believing it all—different!

The outline of this book was originally developed when I was asked by an Episcopal priest, a colleague and friend, to share how it was that I came to be a "different Baptist," thinking more broadly than most Baptists he encountered, having ventured into the terrain of a progressive/liberal theology. As I considered his invitation, I reflected on the influences that had subtly, imperceptibly at the time, changed the trajectory of my faith while rooting me even more solidly in the career I first sensed as a first-grader who wanted to be a preacher "like my daddy."

It was an interesting, profitable exercise. I encourage you to try it. What simple experiences, what people, what event, maybe represented by a single sentence or phrase or insight, opened up new avenues of growth for you? Perhaps this journey through my own reflection will be helpful to you, but undertaking your own reflection would be even more meaningful.

As I begin this reflection about the experiences that have led me away from much of the theology of my childhood home, and circuitously back home, I would be remiss, even downright wrong, not to begin in the actual home of my childhood. It was there that it all began. Without that home, the nurturing and encouragement of parents deeply rooted and committed to their own faith, my journey would not have been possible. While the challenges, the questions, the doubts that have accompanied the kind of faith that is all important to me now were blissfully removed from the experience of my home, I believe the seeds of that growth were planted there.

My mother says I asked a zillion questions as a child, but I don't remember asking a single question of faith that was not satisfied with a rather simple answer—until I reached college (see ch. 2). However, in the honesty of my parents' answers, the integrity of their practice, the sincerity of the faith they still live by, I experienced *active* faith, and this "movement" of their convictions prepared me by sharing a foundation that would "go the distance." The terrain varied over these years, but there was always ground beneath my feet.

I might characterize the nature of my childhood faith as "devotional" or "personal." By that I mean that it was not a dry, intellectual exercise, and never divorced from the heartfelt experiences of growing up and family and the lessons of life. I am grateful to have had such an introduction to the life of faith. If the famous scholar and missionary Albert Schweitzer knew faith to be that "longest journey from the mind down to the heart,"[5] my experience took the opposite tack. It began within, in the stirrings of the spirit, in the *feelings* of faith practiced within family and community.

Both of my parents studied at The Southern Baptist Theological Seminary,[6] my mother in the Christian education program, my father finishing with a divinity degree. They came from small South Carolina towns, raised in Baptist churches that were formative and supportive. My childhood home and church, my "raising," represented everything that was good about the Southern Baptist Convention (SBC). Though I have little respect for the fundamentalist leanings of the denomination in its current form, the SBC was great for my parents, and it was a good home for my siblings and me as a child.

Each evening in the Dean home, when my mother tucked her three children to bed, she always paused to offer a devotion of some kind. She would read a Bible story or a verse or ask about our day, and we would always say a prayer. She would pray and also ask us to speak our own prayers, which was a helpful introduction to the public praying that apparently awakens many adults with night terrors! My earliest memories of these devotions go back to the two-story brick parsonage owned by the May Memorial Baptist Church in Powhatan, Virginia. As I remember that house, I see it set on a hill at the top of what seemed like a mile-long asphalt driveway, where I learned to ride a bicycle. The woods behind the house provided the perfect roaming grounds for the adventures of two young brothers.

But as I remember that house, it is a sound that stands symbolically for my childhood experience. The sound is my mother's singing. It's not the voice of a trained soprano that still runs through my soul, but a warbled, inconsistent melody, the pitch wavering falteringly. The stream of audible air may not have passed through highly refined vocal folds, but they resonated from one heart to another, and I'm still touched when she sings from my distant memory: "Into my heart, into my heart, come into my heart, Lord Jesus. Come in today. Come in to stay. Come into my heart, Lord Jesus."

Those words perfectly reflect the evangelical fervor of the Southern Christianity I was bequeathed. Faith was about accepting Jesus into your heart and letting him be Lord and Savior. These words, perhaps ironically, still resonate in my *heart*, and they are the perfect companion to the seeking *soul*, the liberal *mind*, and the sometimes-frail-but-always-energetic *strength* that also characterize my love for God (Mark 12:30). It all began by asking Jesus to come "into my heart," and while the mileposts of my journey indicate that I've traveled a long way down the road and passed many landmarks that would not have been recognizable in my childhood, faith is still deeply personal, personally devotional for me.

As Amy and I share the preaching load at Park Road Baptist Church, our congregation has come to expect two emotions from our pulpit: When she preaches, people in the congregation have a tendency to cry. She speaks from the heart, tells stories, shares a mother's intuition, and her style often tugs on people's tears. When I preach, I'm often working out some theological idea, digging at a scriptural phrase or a biblical concept, stereotypically preaching from the head, where Amy preaches from the heart. Ironically, the emotional expression generated by my preaching generally comes from the preacher! While I don't cry when I preach, it's not at all uncommon for me to have to pause, sometimes at the most unexpected times, to gather my composure. Those ideas I preach and teach, far from being cold or sterile, academic exercises removed from my heart, are deeply entwined in it. Head and heart go together in faith.

As Amy and I have ventured into more liberal theological terrain in our preaching and teaching, reading and studying, we have noticed that the journey into more liberal terrain does seem to cause some people to lose the joy of faith. Proper faith, as it were, becomes critical faith, rejecting faith, "deconstructing" faith. The wife of a young couple who joined our church some years ago had completed two years of seminary in another city. When we spoke with them about her experience, she recalled for us the excitement of seminary, but the disrupting, dislocating disappointment that it also brought: "I got deconstructed in seminary—but never reconstructed again!"[7]

These experiences of "deconstruction" and "reconstruction" are evident in the language of some Christians and in various books by Christian writers. Some seem intent to deconstruct—to break down everything, sometimes to the extreme of rejecting faith altogether ("throwing the baby out with the bathwater"). Others who have engaged this journey, while sharing much of the theology of the "deconstructors," are able to express the need to analyze, to critique, to deconstruct while maintaining the joy of faith. Deconstruction should lead to reconstruction. Critique can lead to celebration. Tearing down must lead to rebuilding—if we remain true to the discipline of faith.

This has been my experience. While I can speak of a crisis, or maybe *crises*, of faith, and while the road has been winding and filled with potholes and bumps, steep climbs, and unexpected turns, I have never lost my joy. The heartfelt touch of faith that began with those nighttime devotions and a childlike trust that invited Jesus and the whole life of faith to come "into my heart" are still central to my journey.

Thanks for joining me.

Believing in Jesus: Proclamation or Practice?

Matthew 16:13–20

Russ Dean, August 25, 2002

The preacher asked, "What animal is small, brown, and has a large, furry tail?" All of the children gathered around for the Sunday morning children's time stared back with blank faces. "You know," he continued, "it's a small animal with a large, furry tail that likes to eat nuts." Again, blank looks. After a third description one boy in the back of the group sheepishly raised his hand and said, "Well, preacher, I know the answer is 'Jesus,' but it sounds a lot like a squirrel to me!"

Perhaps we don't talk as much about him as some Baptist churches, but I never thought that as a Baptist preacher I would ever be confused or conflicted or concerned about preaching a sermon about *Jesus*. But until a few years ago I never knew there was a Baptist church in the world like Park Road Baptist Church! The truth is, I must confess, Amy and I have been a little confused and conflicted and concerned on this score since before we even became your pastors. Of our immediate predecessor, someone told us as we did our homework about you, "I think he talked about Jesus a little *too much* for them." (What did that mean?) Then we met Charlie Milford, the founding pastor of this church, who for thirty-two years led this congregation in a relentless if unorthodox pursuit of Truth.[8] We had learned that Charlie was, by reputation, an iconoclast, a renegade Baptist in the liberal tradition of the late Carlyle Marney.[9] In our first conversations Charlie spoke (as he still does) often, freely, devotedly of *Jesus*, his prayers ending, always, in the way that only Charlie can say it, "In Jeeesus's name."

Not long after arriving on the scene here, to add to our conflict, we were at lunch with one of you whom we have come to trust and respect greatly, and I heard the very unlikeliest of all Baptist declarations of faith: "Well, I don't *believe* in *Jesus*. I *believe* in *God*." In those simple but profound words all that I had learned about Jesus to that point in my life went flying through my head in one of those dizzying my-life-just-flashed-before-my-eyes kind of blurs. In that affirmation of sincere and deeply held faith—"I don't *believe* in *Jesus*. I *believe* in *God*"—twenty centuries of official ecclesiastical wrestling over the person of Jesus of Nazareth flashed before us, and again, Jesus spoke, this time to me: *Who do you say that I am?*

The story of Peter's confession of Christ has been central for the followers of Jesus since it began to circulate, first by word of mouth among his extended band of disciples,[10] then, after his death, among the growing house-churches which sprang up around the ancient world. *You are the Christ*, said Peter, and the confession of one brash and bold believer, as for countless other disciples-become-martyrs, became his last breath.

Who do you *say that I am?*

Some scholars believe that the earliest known formal "confession of faith" (statement of belief) was used in early baptismal liturgies. At baptism a candidate would be charged: "Confess your faith." The candidate would respond in a compact, three-word liturgical formulation of Christian belief: *Jesus is Lord* (Phil 2:11). Amy and I adopted from a colleague and friend his method of carrying on this tradition. In baptism here we ask our candidates to write a brief statement of their faith, which can be spoken for them. Many of you will recall Molly Caldwell's moving poem,[11] which I read before she was immersed. It is our way of invoking a personal "confession of faith" from those who go through these waters.

The statement of the early church was simple but profound: "What do you believe?"

Jesus is Lord.

But moving through the Gospels, in John's narrative, the resurrected Jesus appears to Thomas (the doubter) and extends an offer for Thomas to examine his wounds and, by doing so, to believe. And Thomas's affirmation, as John tells it, now moves well beyond Peter's declaration. Thomas's affirmation is filled with theological premises as well, for his cry names Jesus "my Lord, *and my God*."[12]

For many thinking, discerning believers around the world, it is quite a leap—an unacceptable leap, in fact—to move from a confirmed commitment to Jesus as Lord to this affirmation. To be fair I must say that certainly not all "thinking, discerning believers" have such difficulty. Hardly is this the case. But when we last sang "When I Survey the Wondrous Cross," I heard from some of *you*, for whom the second stanza would not go down too easily:

Forbid it, then, that I should boast,
save in the death of *Christ, my God*;
All the vain things that charm me most
I sacrifice them to Christ's *blood*.[13]

Here is the crux of the issue: We have just come from a study of the Commandments, which begin with the affirmation of one God and a strong prohibition against worshiping anything or anyone but this God. Last week we considered Jesus's own understanding: that the greatest command is to love God *alone*. So we must ask: Is Jesus "Lord"—one to whom we can devote our thinking, our understanding, our priorities, our commitment, our lives in the service of God? Or was Jesus actually God? Was Jesus the *image of the invisible God* (Col 1:15), who, as we follow him, becomes *our way, our truth, our life* (John 14:6) in God? Or is Jesus himself to be praised, sung to, prayed to, *worshiped* as God?

For most of my life, I would have answered the latter, without reservation—without even knowing that there was any other option. Jesus *was* "God in a bod," as someone has put it, rather crassly.[14] The creeds pronounce this faith: "fully human and fully divine," "begotten, not made," "true God of true God." There is plenty of scripture to call as a prooftext, for sure, and more than ample orthodox teaching to bolster the claim. There are thousands of books and millions of believers worldwide who've never given it another thought.

Who do you *say that I am?*

Let's think again.

Hear me carefully, please. I'm not asking you to forsake your faith. I'm not asking you to reject your past. I'm not even asking you, necessarily, to *change* what you believe.[15] I am asking you to think with us, together this fall, as we examine some of Jesus's words and deeds from Matthew's Gospel. I am asking you to think critically and without fear, to examine openly, with twenty-first century minds, the mind of a first-century Jewish peasant who comes to us by way of first-century, mostly Jewish documents[16] and almost twenty centuries of religious devotion. I am asking you to sit among his disciples, to look into his eyes, to hear again his world-changing question: *Who do* you *say that I am?*

There is a feud going on in the world of academia about this question that Jesus asked. This feud has been dubbed the "Jesus Wars." In 1985 an academic named Robert Funk called together a band of New Testament scholars to study the words of Jesus of Nazareth as found in the Gospels. The "Jesus Seminar" began evaluating all of the sayings of Jesus, using critical literary tools, and by so doing sought to get back to the supposed "real" or "historical Jesus," whom they believed was distinct from the Jesus of a simple, literal reading. Their so-called "Quest for the Historical Jesus" actually began in the mid-1800s. Scholars had begun to notice various "layers" within the Scripture, which they believed could be determined by a complex study of word usage and grammatical constructions (among other things). In peeling back these layers, most scholars have come to agree that the Gospel of Mark was written first and that Matthew and Luke both knew and used Mark (as well as another common source[17]) in writing their narratives. According to this theory, the Gospel of John was the last book written, and John's glorious language reflects the theological development within the church between the death of Jesus and approximately 100 C.E.[18]

Due to the use of this method,[19] some scholars believe that much of what we know of Jesus in the Gospels is not true to who he actually was as a person. In this view, in the years after Jesus's death, the church, reflecting on his life and developing a theology distinct from its Jewish roots, increasingly edited the oral stories and read onto Jesus's lips their growing understanding of a God who could be physically present among them with life-giving, life-changing force. In this view many of the "red-letter words" of Jesus cannot be known decisively to have come from his own mouth. In this view also, many of the deeds of Jesus, especially his miracles, are questionable as "historical" events and are read instead as metaphorical or mythological stories, pointing to a truth deeper than the actual "factuality" of the event.[20]

The two quotations given as our opening meditation[21] indicate perhaps the two extremes in this war over Jesus. Either he was literally who the Scripture says he was, or the image revealed in Scripture is a "Christ of faith," who *may* have been quite different from the "Jesus of history."

The work of the historical-critical method, which I have briefly summarized for you, has influenced nearly all who study the Bible today, from the far left to the far right. Its importance can hardly be overestimated. And this most current "Quest for the Historical Jesus" is fascinating to study. We have much to learn about Jesus from this approach.

But as revealing and important as this approach is to our biblical understanding, ultimately, the questions of the Jesus Seminar are useless. For Jesus did not ask Peter, and he does not ask us, *Who do you say that I was?* The God of Jesus was not a God of the dead, but of the living,[22] not a God of the past but of the ever-renewing present. And according to Marcus Borg, himself one of the participants in the Jesus Seminar, Jesus is, ultimately, "not simply a figure of the past, but a figure of the present. Meeting that Jesus—the *living Jesus* who comes to us even now—will be like meeting Jesus again for the first time."[23]

I see the series of pictures as some kind of out-of-body experience. I am about ten years old…

Sitting at the foot of my parents' bed, talking with my father, asking how to "let Jesus come into my heart."

I am there now, clutching the rail of the pew in front of me, waiting for stanza one to begin. I am stepping out, seeing my father's face, holding his hand, feeling his arms around my shoulders, hearing his voice in my ear.

Finally, I am in the water, deep, warm, clear. And again, my father's voice: "Because of the divine command of our Lord and Savior, Jesus Christ, and because of your profession of faith in him, I baptize you my son…."

Marcus Borg, a boy who gave his heart to Jesus and who became a liberal interpreter of the faith, says, "[I've] been 'looking for Jesus all [my] life.'"[24] His story is my story. The quest for Jesus is a journey for a lifetime. In my own search for the "real Jesus," I have learned some appropriate distinctions.

I no longer simply equate Jesus and God, but I do regard the relationship between God and Jesus, and Jesus's own life in God, as *unique*.

I believe that the Gospels evidence some progression or development in their portrayal of Jesus. I think we should listen carefully to what this progression might tell us about Jesus, about the church, about ourselves. But I do not despair over the unsolvable quest for who he *was* in history, and I do not abandon the faith of my childhood nor disdain the belief of the majority of Christian believers who do not share my views.

I consider the life, death, and resurrection of Jesus Christ to be *essential* in my understanding and appropriation of faith.

"In both Greek and Latin [to believe] means to 'give one's heart to.' The 'heart' is the self at its deepest level."[25] Believing is not just claiming something in our head, then; it is seeking to *practice* it in all that we do. I do *believe* in Jesus. I believe not because I proclaim what the Gospels say happened outside of Jerusalem some 2,000 years ago as salvation. I believe in Jesus because I believe that in *practicing* his compassion, in *practicing* his commitment, in *practicing* his kind of godly love, in knowing his mind and sharing his heart, like him, I can come to know what it means to be fully human.

And they say, "Practice makes perfect."

May it be so.

LET US PRAY: "I Believe in God because I believe in Jesus. Or more probably, [without Jesus] God simply would not matter. The story of Jesus enables me to envision God as One who genuinely cares for each and all of us. In Jesus, God confronts the Darkness face to face, Incarnate, for our sake. Jesus is Light to the gentle face of God. The story of Jesus says that God laughs with us in our joys and weeps with us in our sorrow. God strengthens us in the helplessness of our hoping, God stands with us in the uncertainty of our believing, and God waits for us in our yearning to be loved. Ultimately the lonely companionship of Jesus in the suffering of his passion [makes] my painful journey a sometime story of faith."[26]

(SUNG)
Jesus, Jesus, how I trust him.
     How I've proved him o'er and o'er.
Jesus, Jesus, precious Jesus.
     O for grace to trust him more.[27]

Amen!

The Baptism of Molly Caldwell

By Molly Caldwell

I take one last breath held in with faith
Then succumb to Your gentle wave of righteousness,
Fall into Your ocean of freedom, glimmering with hope.
In You I trust, You will fill me up, You will make me whole.
Thru the storm You salvaged me, You were my beacon
When there was no light to be seen.
And now You have shined upon me,
For that I shall be fruitful.

Deliver me unto Your grace.
Allow me to resonate in Your goodness.
Let all that You embody seep to the heart,
And once I am refreshed, washed in Your glory
I will then offer it back to You.
May Your will engulf me.

Submerge me in Your strength and peace,
So I shall walk out anew

And before Your might of all that's true
I'll raise my head and wake to dream
I will walk thru these waters and come out clean
May Your residue cling to me

Printed with permission of the author.

Notes

[1] T S. Eliot, Anne Hodgson, and Philip Mairet, *Little Gidding* (London: Faber and Faber, 1942), 59.

[2] Years ago, somewhat by happenstance, Amy and I began closing our sermons with these words. It happens routinely now. Some in our congregation are not aware of the meaning behind our tradition, but the word *Amen* means, literally, "may it be so," so this parting word is intended to end our sermon with the prayerful hope that what we've delivered might have been insightful or challenging or comforting enough as to have been a word from God, and that the message will not end in the speaking or the hearing but in the "may it be so—of our own lives."

[3] My friend, the late Dr. William E. Hull, spoke of faith in this way.

[4] The quotation, "The job of the newspaper is to comfort the afflicted and afflict the comfortable," was originally spoken by a fictional bartender named Mr. Dooley, introduced in 1893 by Finley Peter Dunne, who wrote for the *Chicago Evening Post.*

[5] This quotation comes from Kyle Matthew's 2016 song "My Argument" (*Waking Up to the World,* by See For Yourself Music). According to Kyle, this quotation is based on an interview once given by the late Albert Schweitzer.

[6] Throughout the book I will refer to Southern Baptist Theological Seminary by a number of names: Southern Seminary, Southern, and SBTS.

[7] *Deconstruction* is jargon specific to academic theology, which refers especially to breaking down the stories of Scripture, "deconstructing" or "demythologizing" them in an effort to look for a deeper meaning. The miracles of Jesus, for example, are demythologized, the miraculous events rejected as incredible to the modern, scientific mind. After deconstructing the "miracle" itself, a deeper truth emerges (i.e., a change to the disciples' faith, a lesson learned, a truth empowered, etc.). Sadly, our friend is not the only one to have experienced a near loss of faith when this academic discipline results in "throwing the baby out with the bathwater!"

[8] Charlie's phrase, "Truth is more a becoming than a having," might well characterize his ministry as a whole. Through sermons and Bible study opportunities, Charlie's ministry was defined by an open, spirited, ongoing debate with his congregation. No questions or theological issues were off-limits in this conversation. He saw this as essential in leading his congregation to a proper understanding of Christianity.

[9] Carlyle Marney served Myers Park Baptist Church in Charlotte for many years and was a close personal friend of Charlie Milford.

[10] I believe there were many disciples, though the New Testament names only twelve as "apostles."

[11] I have included Molly's poem at the conclusion of this sermon.

[12] John 20:28. We should recognize that from a more conservative perspective, there is no "distance" at all between the confessions of Peter and Thomas. "Jesus is Lord," in a more traditional

understanding, implies the same route to divinity as does Thomas's more explicit claim. I do believe, however, that some theological development is discernible within Scripture (from the Old Testament to the New Testament and within each Testament itself).

[13] Isaac Watts, "When I Survey the Wondrous Cross," 1707.

[14] The statement was made by Dr. Molly T. Marshall in a lecture given in class at Southern Baptist Theological Seminary. "It is *not enough*," she said, "just to say that Jesus is 'God in a Bod.'"

[15] I walk a fine line here. It is my hope that in preaching and teaching, people will change what they believe. It has been because of my changed beliefs, due to careful teaching and nudging, that my faith has become what it is. I do seek this kind of change for other people, but I recognize the "careful" nature in which this must be done, and I believe that our theological positions are not as important as our convictions in faith-in-action. So I am content for people to believe very differently if we can agree to live and work together in peace.

[16] The New Testament culture was Jewish, so even the later Epistles, written from a fully Christian perspective, must be understood from this culture.

[17] This source can be "seen" by observing the material common to Matthew and Luke, which shares common vocabulary, syntax, etc. Scholars call this hypothetical source "Q," for the German *quelle*, meaning "source."

[18] Out of respect for sisters and brothers who are not of the household of Christian faith, I have adopted a convention of calendaring that does not center time around the event of Jesus Christ. Rather than "B.C." (before Christ) and "A.D." (*Anno Domini*, "in the year of the Lord"), I have accepted the designations "B.C.E." (before the common era) and "C.E." (common era).

[19] The historical-critical method was developed in the mid-1800s.

[20] Luke Timothy Johnson's critically acclaimed work *The Real Jesus: The Misguided Quest for the Historical Jesus and Truth of the Traditional Gospels* (San Francisco: HarperSanFrancisco, 1996) discounts much of the work of the Jesus Seminar and its proponents as theologically biased and unfaithful to well-established methods of scholarly research. See, especially, chapter two, "History Challenging Faith."

[21] "You must make your choice. Either this man was, and is, the Son of God, or else a madman or something worse. You can shut him up for a fool, you can spit at him and kill him as a demon or you can fall at his feet and call him Lord and God." [C. S. Lewis, *Mere Christianity* (London: Collins, 1952), 54–56. (In all editions, this is Bk. II, Ch. 3, "The Shocking Alternative.")]

"Could it be that Christians have done precisely what Jews feared might be done, idolized Jesus of Nazareth? Have Christians supplanted God by deifying Jesus, which is actually the opposite of incarnation? Have Christians taken the way to God and made him a dead end, leading nowhere beyond himself? Has this been done because Christians refuse to live with the holy mystery that is God? Finding it so much easier to get our minds around this Jesus, have we settled for a sentimentalized version of God? Remember, Jesus did not come to found a religion; he came to awaken faith in God." [Gene Owens, *Confessions of a Religionless Christian* (Nashville, TN: Abingdon Press, 1975), 27.

[22] Matthew 22:32.

[23] Marcus Borg, *Meeting Jesus Again for the First Time*, (New York: HarperCollins Publishers, 1994), 137.

[24] Ibid., 6.

[25] Ibid., 137.

[26] Frank Tupper, *A Scandalous Providence* (Macon GA: Mercer University Press, 1995), 19.

[27] Louisa Stead, "Tis So Sweet to Trust in Jesus," 1882.

A New Crisis: Once You Get Educated, Nothing Is Ever Easy Again

Questions to Consider

Do you have any doubts about God? Jesus? The Bible? Faith? Do your doubts worry you?

After your formative education about faith (often through children's Sunday school programs in church), how did your understanding of faith change (if it has)?

Have you ever had an experience that challenged the basic beliefs of your faith? Have you ever had a "crisis of faith"?

Is what you believe about the content of faith essentially the same as what you first learned (whether you still believe it or not)? Think about the math you learned in elementary school, the rules of English, the science, history, social studies. Do you still think about these subjects in the same way, now, as an adult?

What is the difference between *faith* and *belief* (or *beliefs*)?

If what you believe about God is different than what you believed as a child, what has actually changed? You? Your thoughts? Has God changed?

❖

From the cowardice that does not face new truth,
From the laziness that is contented with half-truth,
From the arrogance that thinks it knows all truth,
Good Lord, deliver me. Amen.
—an anonymous Kenyan prayer

As a child, one of those formative stories I learned was about the prophet Samuel. Born of miraculous circumstances to a previously barren mother, Samuel was raised in the church, by the church, because when his mother discovered her surprising pregnancy, Hannah promised her boy to God. Samuel was raised by old Eli, who lived and performed his priestly functions in what I imagine was a cavernous, cold, candle-lit temple at Shiloh, and it was there one night that Samuel heard the voice of God.

Maybe I liked that story because I could relate to it. I, too, was raised in the church, by the church, for the church. It was in the church that I, too, "heard" God's voice. I can hardly imagine a better childhood. I've often said that my parents could have been poster children for the SBC. Everything that was good about the SBC of old was good to them and for them—and I was a beneficiary of the convention's largesse. From curricula to programs to the highly subsidized seminary education I received, the church that raised me was a caring parent. It was also a careful, protective, patronizing parent.

The first church Amy and I served was the First Baptist Church in Clemson, South Carolina. Charles Arrington had been a longtime pastor there, and though he had "found his reward" many years before we began serving his church, in some ways it still had the feeling of being "his church." There are some pastors who are just like that. Their influence far outlives them. Their aura is faintly palpable as you walk the halls, stand in the pulpit, examine faith and theology with people who had known their influence personally. Charles Arrington was that kind of pastor. I think I know why.

When we were living there, one of Dr. Arrington's adult daughters returned to Clemson for a visit. She told me about her father and shared a remarkable story. When she had graduated from high school and was preparing to launch out on her own with a college career, her father sat her down for a conversation. Among the things he told her was a particularly daring pastoral and parental instruction about faith. "When you go away from here," he said, "I want you to *forget everything* you learned here. And I want you to learn it all again—for yourself this time."

Wow. That was *not* the instruction I got from my parents nor from the denominational "parents" who produced programs and literature for the Baptist churches they served. In fact, when we went off to Southern Seminary to get our own education, someone warned Amy and me of the dangers of that education: You know, it's okay to go up to seminary and take classes and get a degree—but don't let seminary change what you really believe (this is what she actually said). For a lot of folks, apparently all you really need to know is what you learned in kindergarten Sunday school class. The basic stories, the simplest meaning—those are enough. And don't you forget it!

I do not intend to demean the childhood I experienced nor the faith education I received—quite the opposite. Again, I cannot imagine a better foundation. The problem is that the purpose of a foundation is to provide the structure for the (more important) building—while the foundation I received seemed to be understood as the structure itself. The basic stories, with the simplest, most child-friendly explanations (and what else do you give a child?), were understood to be adequate—adequate explorations of a rich literary source and adequate justifications for the adult.

No one ever encouraged me to forget what I had learned—*as a means of challenging me* to go deeper, as a means of making the faith of my parents and church *my own faith*. I only recently discovered this fascinating text from the sixth chapter of the book of Hebrews, though I believe Charles Arrington was channeling those biblical words perfectly: *Therefore, let us go on toward perfection* leaving behind *the* basic teaching *about Christ* (Heb 6:1).

Forget everything you learned; learn it all again—for you this time.

There was a fearful, parochial sense about God and the world in my early faith. Faith was not supposed to open us up to the increasingly difficult questions of life, the very real challenges of adulthood. Faith, if understood simply and lived blindly, would protect us from these. Faith should shield us from these challenges. In fact, just knowing those kinds of questions existed (the questions that invariably challenge faith) was a kind of proof that one did not have enough faith.

I learned this proof all too well my freshman year at Furman University. "Intro to philosophy" was a cruel teacher.

The student body at Furman was mostly conservative. The university was still tied to the Southern Baptist Convention in the 1980s, so many students wore purple because of their Baptist background. Being located just on the edge of the foothills of the South Carolina mountains provided a conservative ethos (it was just in the air). A conservative politic also pervaded much of the student spirit. In this environment, quickly finding myself in a Christian crowd through the Baptist Student Union and friends from an on-campus "Christian fraternity," I was warned early in my freshman year to stay away from the "liberal religion department" and the philosophy professors ("they're atheists, you know").

I was keen to the warnings about dangerous religion, and I'd never met an atheist, but they probably frightened me more than *A Nightmare on Elm Street*, so I took note. I did take the required "intro to New Testament" that first semester with wary eyes—which shot wide open the day my professor called Antiochus Epiphanes "a real son of a bitch,"[1] but I mostly made it through New Testament with my Sunday school Bible still intact.

Toward the end of that semester, however [cue the ominous music], my friend, Kyle Matthews, who would become a roommate and lifelong friend, said he was signing up for philosophy. "Take it with me," he urged casually, as the best tempters usually do. I reminded him of the caution I had received from my other Christian friends. Kyle shared none of their fear. He said something about challenge being a good thing for faith—something about a new view helping us see with new eyes. He reeled me in. Smoothly. Slowly. Like sheep to the slaughter. I signed up.

Three months later I was living to regret my apostasy.

Someone cued the music when Kyle lured me into this sin, but it wasn't long into that semester that those haunting sounds crescendoed from the low, bass warning (think the movie *Jaws*) to the screeching violin treble (think of the Hitchcock thriller *Psycho*)—and I was the unwary victim! Dr. Douglas MacDonald walked with a cane and would hobble into class every day, perch himself awkwardly on the front of his desk, wrap one leg impossibly around the other, and start, ever so carefully, callously disassembling my faith (just like they told me he would). The method was cruelly casual.

Truth? What is truth? How do you know? Who told you it was "true"? How do *they* know? The Bible? The Bible is true because the Bible says it's true? Isn't that circular logic? Over the years, as Kyle and a few other friends remembered the old philosopher's method, we would recall his debilitating questions with increasing exaggeration, finally growing his legend into our favorite, sarcastic scenario: "Love? What is love? Let's say that young Sara and I are engaged in a relationship" (pointing to the horrified freshman coed sitting to his left). Dr. MacDonald never said that, of course, but we were no less mortified by the questions he *did* ask!

The onslaught lasted an entire, withering, wearying semester. Accompanied by the discussions in class (all of my classmates had obviously not been raised Southern Baptist), the material I was reading that extended Dr. MacDonald's awkward questions with thoughtful, reasonable justifications and the dawning awareness in the pseudoadult setting called college that I really was, pretty much, on my own, I awoke to the startling realization that I was no longer certain what I believed. Oh. My. God. (God?)

The key word here is *certain*. I still had beliefs. The good professor had not been able to strip my beliefs from me, but his method and his madness *had* taken away the certainty of those beliefs. Given my understanding at the time, though, uncertainty was almost equivalent to unbelief. Maybe it was worse:

*"I would thou wert cold or hot. So then because thou art lukewarm, and neither
cold nor hot, I will spue thee out of my mouth"* (Rev 3:15–16 KJV; I could quote
too much KJV scripture for my own good!).

I was not prepared. No one had told me that the real journey of faith
always required *"forgetting what lies behind and straining forward to what lies
ahead"* (Phil 3:13). There was no room for *"leaving behind the basic teaching
about Christ"* (Heb 6:1) in order to move forward. So I found myself in a new
land and was unmoored…drifting…doubting…reeling.

I may have even said it out loud, this feeling that was burning me up
inside: "Why did I go and screw up such a good thing? I had the answers. I
should *never* have taken this class, asked these questions!" And I knew that I
could not go back. I had let the cat out of the bag, opened a can of worms,
pried the lid off of Pandora's box. It was the end of my innocence, and, looking back on it, it feels so "textbook" as to be worthy of more hackneyed clichés
than you can shake a stick at!

At the moment, however, it was no laughing matter. I was afraid. I don't
know if I thought I actually might have lived a life free from such struggles if
I had never stepped into that syllabus, but I was sure that there was no way
to get back there. Before the days of GPS, someone stopped in a small town
to ask for direction and was told, flatly, "No…you can't get there from here!"
Well, that illogic was absolutely true for this college freshman. Once you've
crossed that threshold, you, literally, cannot go back. While I was still mostly
naïve about most of the world, I had an intuitive sense of this deep truth.

At the time I could not see that the faith I would cultivate in the years to
come would be deeper and stronger than the faith I lost. At the time I did not
know that what I had called *faith* may have been little more than rote belief.
At the time I could not see that *my* faith was probably just the faith of my
parents or my church or my friends; only in the "forgetting" that philosophy
had provoked would that faith ever really become mine. At the time I just
knew that everything had changed, and in that moment I knew that it would
never be easy again.

Since that moment the life of faith has grown beyond what I could have
imagined. It has become a source of strength I could not have handled at
the time. It has opened me to a God of depth and texture I could never have
conceived. It has introduced me to a world of Truth through different and
differing religious truths. But since that day it has never been easy.

I'm so glad.

Deep into that spring semester I walked into McAlister Auditorium for convocation. Furman had ceased mandatory chapel services and like many universities had begun requiring attendance at a minimum number of "Cultural Life Programs" each semester instead. Someone has said TED Talks are "sermons" for a secular culture (we all need to feed our souls). Universities can pretend they're being sensitive to a pluralistic culture—tending the mind, not catering to religion—and individuals can log on to TED for their "intellectual enrichment" if they need to use that ruse (but it's all the same thing!). That day, in a mostly empty auditorium, the Tennessee farmer/activist Will Campbell was speaking to me—preaching to me. McAlister might as well have hosted an audience of only one that morning because Campbell was on Furman's campus that day for no other reason. He had come that day to say to me, "Once you get educated, nothing is ever easy again."

The fiery, country-voiced prophet had just spoken to the emotion that was tearing at me. It wasn't just sadness or fear or regret or confusion. I had all of those emotions, but when Will Campbell made that simple declaration, I realized that I was, mostly, angry. I was angry at Kyle for enticing me. I was angry at Dr. MacDonald for so rudely awakening me. I was angry at Furman University for promoting a secular education that "enlightens." I was angry at God, though at that point I could not have admitted that (MacDonald had breached the wall of comfortable religion, but he had not taken away the fear of God!). Mostly, though, I was angry at myself. I should have been smarter than this, more resolved, more…faithful.

In the days ahead (okay, maybe it was years!), my anger slowly subsided, however. Other friends and mentors tended my grief. Bits of clarity began to displace the confusion. I forgave Kyle for his complicity with Furman, and I forgave their duplicity with the devil! And though a preacher from Tennessee had not solved my problem, had not given back the certainty a contorted, desk-sitting philosopher had taken from me, he *had* named for me this door I had opened. Naming it helped me know I was not alone. Though that one simple sentence had concisely named my experience, over time it offered me the hope that if others had walked through that door, then I could too. It wasn't like I had any other choice, but knowing there had been others and that I would have companions on a journey back to faith (forward to faith?) gave me an increasing confidence. Naming the pain can have that effect.

I do not use the word *crisis* lightly. There has been no other time in my life that I have felt my faith shaken. It wasn't that I was afraid I would give up my faith, but I could not see any way that the faith that had provided such certainty and comfort, such answers and assurance, could ever be revived. What I learned—and this is what a good crisis will do for you—is that it would not be revived, very much as it should be. *Let the dead bury their dead, Jesus said!* (Luke 9:60).

When someone dies, we grieve, but we gather to speak a good word, to celebrate the life they lived, and we move on. We do not go without them— they are very much with us—but they journey with us in a different way. They are changed. We are changed. We never revive what has been lost, but gradually we replace the old with a new normal. It is said that a man never really becomes a man until his father dies. That loss is, strangely, necessary for growth and maturity. No one would ask for it, but life comes out of death— always and only.

So it was in my crisis of faith. I have not regained what was lost. The faith that was comfortable and easy has not returned—and though it was a difficult lesson to learn, I now know this is as it should be. The faith that was defined by certainty has been replaced with a confident realism. That faith, which was concerned with answers and proof, has given way to a freedom to pursue the questions of a never ending quest of spiritual exploration. The faith that was bequeathed to me by parents and church became uniquely mine.

"Once you get educated, nothing is ever easy again."

It has not been. I'm so grateful.

Everything worth having is worth working for, and this ought to be at least as true for faith as for any other possession. Sometimes it takes a crisis to make you appreciate the work.

THE PARK ROAD PULPIT
SERMONS FROM
PARK ROAD
BAPTIST CHURCH
RUSS AND AMY JACKS DEAN, PASTORS

The Growth of God

Psalm 137:1–4; John 3:8

Russ Dean, September 11, 2005

Over the course of this year, we will study as a congregation "The Church and Social Change," a program developed out of conversations with our deacons. The first of three emphases in this year of study is "Changing Structures of Authority." This sermon served as an introduction to that emphasis, and prior to the sermon, I shared the following words as a qualification of the sermon title and the idea that God "grows."

***

Alfred North Whitehead spent much of his life as a mathematician before turning his attention to theology. The language of the theology he knew was not satisfactory to Whitehead's view of the world, so he set about to offer a new language by which his mathematical, scientific, and technical world could understand God. Whitehead began to conceive of God "not just as an external being, but as a divine process coming into being within the life of this world."[2]

For Whitehead and the followers of his "process theology," contrary to popular understanding, God changed—constantly. God was not the unchangeable power above the world, but the heart of the process of unfolding and becoming that is our world.

I appreciate what I know of process theology, but when I titled my sermon "The Growth of God," I did not have process theology in mind, but something much more practical. I believe the language we use to speak of God creates an image for God, and that image, for all intents and purposes, becomes God. Does God "grow" or change? I like to speculate with the process theologians (though any answer to that question is but speculation), but I am convinced in a much more practical way that the answer is very much "yes"—God "grows" (in the world) through our understandings and actions and language.

***

It could only be described as indescribable. Almost overnight, all was lost. The storm had gathered on the horizon, visible for days, but in a way it had been there, brewing for years. Prophets had spewed tales of impending disaster, but their gloom fell on deaf ears. The force of inertia, which almost always marries itself to a justice of procrastination (you know, "what's not right, we probably can't change anyway, but we'll try to do better...tomorrow"), the *killing* drag of inertia, is almost always insurmountable. The rich are always too comfortable and too self-absorbed to change; the poor are already too downtrodden to get up. So rich and poor, who disbelieved for too long, braced, too late, for the onslaught.

Homes fell under the great wrath. Families were lost, divided by death and separation. The city reeked of disaster. Destruction and disgrace filled the air for weeks. And when the fury subsided, an entire people awoke with nothing but the clothes on their backs. Across a sea of refugees, faces showed the stain of sweat and tears, minds swaggered in empty comprehension, hearts fell flat for want of help and hope, and quietly the questions surfaced: Where is God? Who is God? What is God? Is God?

The story may sound familiar—as in, the only news you've heard for weeks[3]—but the year was 586 B.C.E., and the storm was named Nebuchadnezzar. His Babylonian army blew into Jerusalem with Category V ferocity, and when the calm finally returned, the people knew their city and their lives—and their God—would never be the same again—*for the spirit blows where it chooses.*

The hurricane I have described is known to historians as the Babylonian exile. You cannot understand your Bible without knowing of the two great exiles of the Israelites: the first occurring in Egypt, the second lasting for two generations under the scourge of a Babylonian king. You cannot fully understand the faith Jesus practiced, nor the faith that has become our own, without being aware of these formative moments in Jewish history. And even if you have no interest in biblical history, I believe you cannot understand the winds that are brewing on the horizon of *our world* unless you understand the forces that were at work in this ancient tempest. It was a political and cultural and religious crucible, which reached its melting point on the banks of that foreign river. It was a crucible in which God grew up.

You need not be an historian to understand the exile. You need only remember this (and make whatever contemporary comparison seems apt[4]): At the moment of crisis, the nation of Israel was enjoying nearly unprecedented success. Politically, militarily, economically, and especially *religiously*, the nation *seemed* to be flourishing. Despite the growing cry of a few prophets, the likes of Amos and Hosea and Isaiah; despite their cry that the rich were getting richer and the poor were getting poorer; despite their efforts to show that there was a connection between the two; despite their denouncement of the laws of the land as ungodly for so favoring the "haves" over the "have-nots"; despite their calls to repentance and a return to faithful covenant; despite these voices, which many denounced as the pathetic jeremiads of a liberal elite; despite these few annoying voices, the nation prospered. And remember this about Babylon: It was to such a nation, whose *preachers* had wrapped Israel's success and Israel's prosperity and Israel's election (as "God's chosen") and Israel's cultural and economic way of life and Israel's *religion* in a *divine* seal of approval—it was to such a nation that unimaginable crisis came.

Every time human beings have made such arrogant claims—that God is "*our* God"; that we, and we *alone*, know God's will; that *we* are "in" and *they* are "out"; that *our* understanding is the only true understanding; that our Scripture (or our *understanding* of that Scripture) is the sole bearer of revelation—every single time a people have made such absolute claims, just offshore the winds begin to blow. They are humbling winds, powerful winds, and they brew a storm of divine destruction[5]—*for the spirit blows where it chooses.*

Thanks be to God that in the aftermath of such storms, God always grows up, and though the progress is ever so slow, the growing God brings us along.

Remember this about Babylon: The exile marked a momentous change in the lives of the Israelites, for only at the hands of utter destruction could they finally realize just how narrow had been their vision of life, their interpretation of faith, their image of God. Thanks to what the late John Claypool has called a "ministry of interpretation," the prophet Ezekiel, preaching an unorthodox word—that is, a word contrary to the *prevailing majority opinion*[6]—the prophet Ezekiel offered the people a new faith, a new hope, a new God altogether.

It is frightening to have to give up God.[7] It is disconcerting and disconnecting to part with friends and family because a once-treasured terrain of common faith no longer remains a ground of common convictions. It is frustrating and confusing to give up the trouble-free days of childhood, with its solid ground of easy answers, for the sometimes troubling ground of divine disclosure on the one hand and self-discovery on the other. But as Will Campbell once said, "Once you get educated, nothing is ever easy again!"

But this is *precisely* the story of the people of God. One generation's orthodoxy (that is, the prevailing majority opinion) is, for the next generation, heresy. Tell me that I am wrong. Before the exile God lived, quite literally, in a box inside one room of an ostentatious shrine in the heart of Jerusalem. But in *exile* the people met a *new God*, whose presence and privilege could not be confined.[8] They could hardly be called the same God.

Before Jesus Christ walked among us, God marched with armies and hurled stones of killing destruction; God sent plagues of death and cloaked himself[9] in almighty power. But in *Jesus* the people met a *new God*, whose heart recoiled within, a God who took pain and sin and death within instead of wielding power without.[10] They could hardly be called the same God.

Before Galileo sighted the stars and charted their courses, God created the world for our pleasure, for we were the center of all that existed. But in a *bigger universe* the people met a *new God*, who was less concerned with human welfare alone than with the nurture and care of all the living cosmos. They could hardly be called the same God.

Before Martin Luther King Jr. marched to Selma, God consigned Americans who traced their ancestry to the African continent to drink out of separate water fountains, to ride in the back of buses, to send their children to inferior schools than did European Americans. But after Sunday morning, April 4, 1968….

Do you see where I'm going?[11] Do you see where *we* are going—the human race, that is—though we have to be drug there, kicking and screaming all the way, every single time that God grows up? Do you see where *God* is going—with us?

So many more examples of a growing God could be given—too many more, in fact—so we must ask: How many more shots will have to ring out in the air of the Memphis, Tennessees, of this world? How many more trials of excommunication will have to be held? How many more crosses will have to be raised to torture the Sons of God before we can realize that God is never going back to be the kind of God that God used to be?

Growing is who God is.

The current storm has been called a culture war—and it *is*—for it is pushing us (and I am speaking especially of American Christians) to rethink, again, the shape of our world, its "truths," and its "authorities"; to rethink, again, our very image of God. In that war we hear words like pluralism, family, evolution, homosexuality, genetic engineering, freedom, marriage. I do not know what will become of this war. It frightens me to think how fierce the storm might become. And I do not know what our world will look like when the calm finally comes. But of one thing I am convinced: The God that we have come to know in the face of Jesus Christ *is growing*, if ever so slowly. And I am convinced that after the storm, we will have moved[12] yet another step *toward* inclusion, acceptance, forgiveness, community, dialogue, wholeness, relationship. Which is to say that God is always growing into that which God always is: *Beloved, let us love one another,* for God is love.

The spirit blows where it chooses. Let us welcome the winds and pray that God will grow up again very soon.

May it be so!

Notes

[1] Antiochus was the Seleucid ruler whose ungodly policies finally angered the Jews into rebellion. In 164 B.C.E. he had a pig slaughtered on the altar of the Jerusalem temple, and that was the final straw. The Maccabean Revolt led to a 100-year period of Jewish sovereignty in Israel. So Antiochus was a bad guy, but I was not quite prepared for my professor to use such profanity. (That was not properly Baptist!)

[2] John Shelby Spong, *Why Christianity Must Change or Die* (New York: HarperCollins, 1998), 63.

[3] Hurricane Katrina came ashore in New Orleans, Louisiana, on August 29, 2005, as a Category 3 hurricane near Buras-Triumph, Louisiana.

[4] As I read the Old Testament, especially the eighth-century prophets (such as Amos, Micah, Hosea, Isaiah), I am amazed at the parallels that I see between the culture of Israel and our own. I find that the prophets' warnings are still quite contemporary. This comment does not relate only or specifically to events surrounding Hurricane Katrina.

[5] Following worship my wife said to me, "If I didn't know you, I would have heard this statement as an affirmation that 'God sent Katrina to punish an unfaithful people.'" I did hesitate with the words "divine destruction" because I believe that it is neither in God's will nor in God's power to deliberately control storms. On my understanding of God's power, I would cite my sermon from June 26, 2005, "Grasping at Silk: Everlasting Arms and the Problem of Pain." I settled on "divine destruction" because of the overall emphasis of the sermon: that we cannot control the movement of God (*The spirit/wind blows where it chooses*), and this movement often comes with "destructive" force—uprooting our lives, causing upheaval and great change. See below, "It is frightening to have to give up God."

[6] Many people would disagree with my understanding that orthodoxy is only a "prevailing majority opinion," though I suspect most of these would consider themselves orthodox in their opinions! I allow that there is an implied understanding that orthodoxy comes with God's imprimatur—not simply the vote of a council—but this understanding is tenuous, at best, especially given the many examples of orthodoxy-gone-bad. See, below, the few examples I give of "one generation's orthodoxy."

[7] See John Shelby Spong, *Why Christianity Must Change or Die*, chapter two, "The Meaning of Exile and How We Got There."

[8] See John Claypool's book *Glad Reunion* (Chicago, IL: Insight Press Inc., 2000), especially the chapter on Ezekiel.

[9] Amy and I were trained in the use of inclusive language, and I am a firm believer. I have disabused myself of the use of masculine pronouns to speak of God, but I believe, in reference to this particular image of God, it is appropriate to speak in masculine terms.

[10] I hesitated with this example because, though as a Christian I affirm that Christ most clearly reveals God to us, it is not entirely fair to say that this God, who takes pain within, was unknown to the Jews before Jesus. In fact, I allude to the language of Hosea in this very statement, How can I give you up, Ephraim? "*How can I hand you over, O Israel? My heart recoils within me; my compassion grows warm and tender. I will not execute my fierce anger; I will not again destroy Ephraim*" (Hos 11:8–9). The word for "recoil" (from the Hebrew, which means "affecting God's innards in shattering ways") is the same word used in the Sodom and Gomorrah story, where God destroys (shatters) the city for its sin. Is not God saying here, "I have 'grown up' since I dealt with Sodom?" One ironic point running throughout the sermon is that the God who is "growing up" is the God

who has been with us from the very beginning. Even though Christ reveals to us something "new" about God, the loving, self-sacrificing God "revealed in Jesus" has really been with us since Hosea's prophecy, and, I submit, from the *very beginning*. See below: "God is always growing into *that which God always is:…God is love.*"

[11] I was told after the sermon that in some ways this sermon was too difficult, that I had "assumed too much" of my hearers. I do not doubt that this is the case and accept this as a fair critique of my preaching. Instead of saying, "Do you see where I am going?" perhaps I should have said, "Here is the point." In this week's pastor's column in our newsletter, I addressed this sermon and the point I was hoping to make. I summarized the sermon, this "where I'm going," as follows:

The world can only know "God" by the language we use. So when our understanding changes, we present, literally, a different God to the world. A more "grownup God." We no longer think of God like the Jews in exiled Babylon—that God has "grown up." (We have grown up.)

In every sea change of theological thought, the generation facing the change has feared, and has tried to hold on to, its "old God." These keepers of the status quo have decried impending changes as "heresy." But…*the Spirit moves where it chooses…* and, looking back, a new generation decrees just the opposite. (Slavery, once preached as "ordained of God," is almost universally denounced now as the sin of a misguided generation.)

I do not deny that our world is frightening, that a storm of change is again blowing. How will we face the questions of pluralism and sexual morality and loss of known "authorities"? I am praying that we will face them with courage. Trusting that the God who has "grown up" so many times in the past will do so again. In us And, that God will do so very soon.

[12] I should have said, "We will have been moved"—for the point is that *the Spirit blows where it wills*, moving us to places we would never have gone without the nudge of the Spirit's gentle breeze, or the "divine destruction" of a gale-force hurricane.

A New Commitment: I (Still) Do.

Love may begin a marriage; but love does not make a marriage.
You will ride a wild sea, if you think you can build your marriage
upon your love. In fact, it is exactly the other way around: your love,
eventually, shall be built upon your marriage.

Walter Wangerin, Jr.[1]

❖

For an entire year my sister hounded me. There was a new girl in the high school chorus class, and my sister, who was a senior and the pianist for the choir, was trying to look out for her: "Amy Jacks is so cute, and her father is so strict. Maybe he'll let her go out with you." I still do not know what that means. Maybe she could go out with *me* because I was…the preacher's kid (you know what most people think about preachers' kids!)? I was likely to garner a "yes" from a hard-nosed father because my masculinity was obviously no threat to his vulnerable teenage daughter? Was this supposed to be a compliment?

The hounding continued throughout my junior year and all summer when I was home on the weekends from my work at McCall Royal Ambassador Camp, the Baptist boys' camp in the mountains of South Carolina. The badgering reached its apex on Labor Day Monday as my family was making plans to spend the evening at our small cabin on Lake Greenwood: "Call her, Russ. Call Amy Jacks, and ask her to go with us to the lake."

And so it began: September 5, 1981.

I turned onto A. B. Jacks Road just outside of town and picked Amy up for the twenty-five-minute drive to the lake. We swam, flirted on the dock, had dinner with my family. It lasted all of a few awkward hours, and then I took Amy home. As we pulled into her driveway, rounding an expansive front yard, we were listening to a ballad, the theme song from *Ice Castles*: "Please, don't let this feeling end…." The truth is, I think we were both ready for that feeling to end! It was a first date, but I gave her a goodnight kiss, and tiny though it was, it was audacious—and uncharacteristic for either of us. The die was cast.

Five years later we did it again, this time in front of about 500 people at the First Baptist Church of Clinton, South Carolina. My father, who was also the officiant, said, "You may kiss the bride." Almost thirty-three years later, we're still "I do-ing."

Roman Catholics and other liturgical Christian denominations refer to marriage as a sacrament—an outward sign of an inward grace. I believe that. At fiftieth wedding anniversary celebrations we like to say there is no surer sign of the actual presence of God in our world than in a marriage that lasts half a century. I believe that. And if God had not been a particular presence in five years of dating and the more than three decades of the marriage of Amy Adair Jacks and James Russell Dean II, we would not be together today. We would not be together, much less "so happy together," as the Turtles sang it in 1967. And we would not be raising two now-college-age sons and holding one church together for more than eighteen years, through the apocalyptic waves of a turbulent and divisive twenty-first century. I believe that.

In a draft reading of this manuscript, one of my wise mentors said, "Where is *Amy* in these chapters?" The obvious oversight he had observed caused me to ask the same question. To be sure, Amy is not the only one of my friends who has recognized, with a politely humorous jab, "So where's *my* chapter?" She is, however, the most important of those friends, the most obvious influence who seems to have been neglected. So why *doesn't* Amy have a chapter devoted to her influence on me? The answer is simple: Amy has been there for every single chapter, and as my constant companion and colleague, supporter and spouse, she has been challenged—and changed—with me. Walking with me each step of the way, she has seen me through. Amy doesn't need a chapter, because this is really her story too. We have lived all of this together.

I can hardly remember the kids we were when we went to the lake that first night so long ago. We were idealistic and naïve. Our world was small and simple. Faith was parochial and comforting. And the future…well, we just had no idea!

For many years we have noted that had we not changed *together* over these years, we would not have survived. We certainly would not have survived as a dating and married couple. This chapter, this "parenthesis," is my attempt to pause as I begin, to acknowledge that as I began this journey, Amy was already with me. While at the time she may not have known of the specific words that I am identifying in these chapters (only in retrospect have they come into full view for me), she was part of the story as it was unfolding. Every chapter, every change, Amy was there.

Considering the flow of experiences I am charting in these pages, had there not been a seed of commitment, strong and true, the deep instinct to love one another—and to love loving one another—we would not have even survived chapter one! I do not even know how to be thankful for this. It just happened so naturally, so slowly, so together(ly) that one of us never had a chance to outgrow the other. I believe it was because we could hold on to each other as we "*work*[ed] *out our* [new] *salvation with fear and trembling*" (Phil 2:12–13). Neither of us was ever tempted by brash anger or naïve arrogance to believe we might outgrow God. To keep the metaphor intact, we kept winding the turns together, cresting the hills, walking through the valleys—and the road just kept leading home.

In the first chapter of my challenge, when I was learning that a good education had blown my comfortable little world to smithereens, Amy was still enjoying the protective comfort of an all-encompassing environment (home and church and small town) that did not allow such questions. As Amy tells it, the questions of philosophy that led to the crisis of faith I have just recounted radiated ripples even into our young relationship. A crisis of faith for me hinted a crisis of relationship for us. Amy will tell you, "I remember thinking as we talked on the weekends about all those questions he was being asked and was asking: 'I don't know if Russ is even still a Christian—and that won't do!'"

Along the winding road that I am charting in the book, this was probably the moment we felt the most tension or personal distance. As much as the questions of philosophy were shaking my foundations, my shaken foundation was the source of angst for a teenage girl, who may even in those very early days have decided she was going to be a preacher's wife, living barefoot and pregnant in small-town America. Her awakenings would come later. In a New Testament survey course with Dr. Tom Stallworth at Presbyterian College and at Southern Seminary with Dr. Glenn Stassen's "Biblical Ethics on Christian Peacemaking," her little boat got rocked more than a little bit also. That was a good thing. Her own education was necessary for us both, because if we had not changed together, we would never have survived.

Maybe it was adolescent puppy-love. Maybe it was the seed of the real thing. Whatever it was, why-ever, however, she stayed with me. She didn't understand, but she stayed with me. Until she experienced a similar challenge through her own education, she could only show up, hold on, and hope.

Show up. Hold on. Hope. That's not a bad formula for a successful marriage. So even in those early days, before we made that age-old commitment at an altar of promise, even from "chapter one" we were learning a *new* commitment: I (still) do. Despite the change, I (still) do. Despite the confusion, I (still) do. Despite all that would be new, all the exploration, all the unknown, all the unforeseen…I (still) do.

I got educated—and nothing was ever easy again—but it was easier than it might have been because Amy was there, getting educated with me. We no longer celebrate the easy faith of our childhood, but we have not looked back. Learning together, we have not lost the joy.

I learned a new way to read the Bible, and Amy shared all the new insights with me.

The focus of my faith "did a 180," the orientation shifting completely from there to here, from then to now, from heaven to earth, and Amy stayed in the present tense with me. Our vision came to clearer, nearer focus, together.

I settled in to the new normal of a faith that would always be joyful, even though I also accepted that it would always be a struggle, and Amy still walked with me.

I came to believe that all the lines I had assumed, even the lines of faith and conviction, were arbitrary, drawn of prejudice and perspective, and Amy stepped with me, wary but willing, across borderlines and into the borderland of an ever-expanding grace.

I rethought God from the ground up and abandoned the Church of the Omnipotent Force. In the process I was converted by the presence of limiting love, and Amy had a new encounter with this God too.

I was challenged to think carefully, intently, intentionally, and Amy was there, accepting her own challenge and allowing room for the life of the mind that became so important to me. In doing so she allowed for a head-and-heart approach between us, a feeling-and-thinking dichotomy that may be one of the strengths of our shared pastoral ministry.

I learned that story is the best way to convey truth, that fiction is truer than fact, and Amy helped me appropriate the myth at the heart of all faith stories into our preaching and teaching.

I learned that love without sacrifice is no love at all. I had heard these words, and then Amy taught this truth to me with her own love and blood as she delivered our two sons into this world. The sacrificial love that Jesus says is the heart of God is a life worth embodying—and relying on each other as we feebly pursue this way.

I could not have started this journey at the end and worked backward. I would not have been able to hear. I could not have heard the later lessons, learning their deeper truths, had I not taken the first step and begun slowly.

And I could not have taken the first steps, would not have walked this winding and wonderful way, without Amy. I could not have arrived where I am today without her. I certainly would not be able to call it home. She's been there, literally, from the beginning until this very moment. When I needed to be pushed, she offered the right nudge. When my enthusiasm needed reigning in, she had the right touch to keep me from getting ahead of myself.

When Amy's father died, our older son grieved, "But Pop was the main excitement!" In the home and the ministry that Amy and I have built, those words capture her own spirit. As a wife and mother and homemaker, she has held her three boys together with a deft touch. She's the disciplinarian, the dietician, the director of laughter and entertainment. At Park Road Baptist Church she's the energy, the spirit, and the strength that explains our almost-nineteen years of successful shared pastoral ministry.

At home and at church, she's the main excitement. These words are not to be overly sentimentalized. They don't ooze with romantic hyperbole. It's a simple truth. I have my role to play—and Amy is not perfect, but she plays her role perfectly, and apparently it's the perfect match for mine. We have learned to recognize that often when I'm down, she's up, and when I'm feeling positive and enthusiastic, I get to pick her up. But the energy, the main excitement of what works for us and what works about us, comes from the well of her deep spirit.

I take no credit for the long years we have been together and the success we have enjoyed with marriage and family and career. Nor would I trade my life for another, anywhere on the planet! I don't deserve to be as happy and healthy as she has made us be. Why me? Why us? I do think there has been a special "magic" for us, though the wannabe theologian in me wants to call it providence. For reasons I cannot explain, along a path I could not have predicted—and would not have designed—the challenges have worked for the good. In all of them I have been made stronger. Through each chapter we have become more united.

This is not "Amy's chapter." She is in every one of them. In every challenge, through every change, she has been with me. I love her for that. As the providence of paradoxical timing sometimes works, before we made the *first* commitment, we had already, magically, mystically, miraculously made a *new* commitment.

Thank you, Amy Jacks Dean. I know you do. And the answer is yes: I (still) do (too!).

[1] Walter Wangerin, Jr., "For My Brother Greg on the Occasion of His Marriage to Liza Lachia," *Between Us* (blog) June 9, 2014, https://walterwangerinjr.wordpress.com/2014/06/09/for-my-brother-greg-on-the-occasion-of-his-marriage-to-liza-lachia/.

A New Question:
Looking for the Spirit of the Message

Questions to Consider

How important is the Bible for you? How much do you know it? Read it? Study it?

What does it mean to "know the Bible"? Does that mean being able to quote a lot of verses? Or does understanding the Bible require understanding something about the history of the Middle East, and Greek and Hebrew exegesis, and who wrote the Bible, and about literary criticism?

Do you believe everything in the Bible? Was the world created in six days? Was a man named Jonah swallowed by a large fish, where he lived for three days? Did Jesus raise a dead man named Lazarus from the tomb? Was Jesus resurrected?

Many Christians are raised on a "literal reading" of the Bible. How does such a reading enhance Scripture—and how might such a reading diminish its richness and value?

When the Bible presents stories that contradict some of the basic principles of science (e.g., Jesus walking on the water), how do you read those stories?

How have you learned how to read and understand the Bible—from your parents, from your pastor, from a college-level course of study, from a neighborhood Bible study?

What do you expect from Bible study? Answers? More questions? Inspiration? Truth? New awareness? Insight?

What story do you know that is true, even if it is not historical, factual?

Reflect on this statement: "Just because it didn't happen doesn't mean it's not true."

❖

Most North American Christians assume that they have a right, if not an obligation, to read the Bible. I challenge that assumption. No task is more important than for the Church to take the Bible out of the hands of individual Christians in North America.... Let us rather tell

[our children] and their parents that they are possessed by habits far too corrupt for them to be encouraged to read the Bible on their own.
—Stanley Hauerwas[1]

Apparently I asked a million questions as a child. Apparently I wasn't satisfied with a lot of the answers. Apparently I persisted with a lot of "whys."

Q: "Today is my birthday party! Why is it raining?"

A: "We can't control the weather, Russ. Today is just a cloudy, rainy day."

Q: "Why?"

A: "Well, clouds carry moisture and they bring rain."

Q: "Why?"

A: "Weather patterns, humidity, barometric pressure…the right conditions bring rain."

Q: "Why?"

A: "Because."

Q: "Because why?"

Apparently a lot of my questions related to religious things. I've always been interested in God and the church and the Bible, and I must have wearied my seminary-trained parents, especially nagging my then-stay-at-home mother to death! I never remember questioning a single answer about religion in my childhood. There were no secondary "whys" in my religious questioning. The answers usually ended with, "Well, Russ, the Bible says…." And apparently that was good enough for me. If I had owned a car as a six-year-old, a ten-year-old, a teenager, it might well have been adorned with one of those worn-out bumper stickers proclaiming, "The Bible says it. I believe it. That settles it."

I was a sophomore in college before I asked my first critical religious question. Looking at the story of Moses and Pharaoh in a required course in religion, during class one day we read, "*But the LORD hardened Pharaoh's heart, and he would not let the people go*" (Exod 10:20). Before the disappointing revelation I had that morning in class, the Bible had always made sense, or it had made sense after some rather simple explanation. ("Russ, this was just part of God's plan"; "Russ, God needed to show divine power over the Egyptian ruler"; "Russ, we don't know, but this is what the Bible says, so we cannot question it." Russ: "Oh…okay!")

I don't know what had changed in my head (could it have been intro to philosophy?), but suddenly the words needed to be questioned in a way I had never experienced. "Wait," I thought. "If *God* hardened Pharaoh's heart, wouldn't that sort of make *God* responsible for Pharaoh not letting the people go? And if Pharaoh was not ready to let the people go, so God had to 'convince' Pharaoh by sending plagues and pestilence and pain (and plenty of it) on the people, then wasn't *God*, in a way, *responsible* for that too? And why would... (gulp) God...ever do a thing like that?"

What explanation could possibly suffice? God's will? No. How could pain—such unnecessary, fatal pain—be at all a part of God's will? What "bigger picture" could possibly justify such wrenching human suffering? It wasn't like I lay awake at night dreaming up skeptical, condemning questions like this, so if this question had just come to me, honestly, should I really *not* ask it? Does the Bible teach me to *love God with all [my] mind* (Mark 12:29)? And this text is in the Bible, literally, so...how...and why?

WHY?

Dr. John Shelley, perhaps seeing the first little crack open in the doorway that introduced my mind to a new way of reading the Bible, responded carefully, caringly (as all good professors do). "Sometimes, Russ," he said, "you have to look for the spirit of the Bible's message...not just at the literal words."

"Literal words" and "spirit of the text." Maybe "literal words" *versus* the "spirit of the text"? Dr. Shelley's words jumped out at me. I had never heard anything like that before. It might have been *said*, but I had never heard it.

Wow.

Whereas the crisis of my freshman year unfolded across a slow semester and was resolved even more slowly, Dr. Shelley's words had instant impact. Why this was so, I don't know. Maybe I was just prepared in a way I had not yet been. Maybe that semester in philosophy had done me some good after all. At that moment I was prepared for that door to be opened, and when it opened, there was a ray of light beaming in, like a starburst, leading with streams of illumination, erasing shadows, quenching darkness.

Maybe there is another way to read the Bible.

I'm not sure there's anything our culture needs more than to learn another way to read the Bible. There is a lot of shallow, "bumper sticker theology" in the world ("God said it. I believe it. That settles it!"). A trite approach to life's most difficult questions drives a lot of good, thoughtful people away. Too many have shelved their Bibles altogether and opt for Starbucks on Sundays instead. *The New York Times* and caramel macchiato have become liturgy for a jaded generation. For too many of the remaining folks, that bumper sticker theology is about as far as they get.

It's too bad neither group knows how to read, because the Bible they are missing has an awful lot to say to them both!

Nothing would change the church more than learning to read the Bible anew. Nothing would better mediate the "culture war" that is raging in this country than a good course in biblical literacy. Stanley Hauerwas, the inimitable Duke ethicist, makes the point in a slightly different, and typically Hauerwasian, fashion:

> Most North American Christians assume that they have a right, if not an obligation, to read the Bible. I challenge that assumption. No task is more important than for the Church to take the Bible out of the hands of individual Christians in North America.... Let us rather tell [our children] and their parents that they are possessed by habits far too corrupt for them to be encouraged to read the Bible on their own.[2]

Hauerwas is making a specific point related to American culture and the engagement of the church in the political arena, and his point is well-taken. Many American Christians just assume they should and can read the Bible on their own, for themselves, with no help from anyone. Many have never considered that some literary and theological background is actually needed to understand this book. We distribute Bibles to our third-graders also, but Hauerwas makes an interesting observation. There is an implicit message in that practice: Third-graders are fully capable of reading the Bible. Really?

What if, instead of giving Bibles to children, we continued to tell them the stories, made sure our children knew all the basic characters, plotlines, names, places. Then, when our children reached (maybe) high school, what if we introduced them to an age-appropriate two- or three-year course in biblical and literary criticism? The course could carefully introduce the use of symbolism, allegory, and metaphor, and the importance of narrative. Then, when they graduated from high school, as they were making their way into the real world, what if we gave them a Bible *then*?

I remember my first real Bible (not those children's picture Bibles, but the real thing!). It was a birthday gift when I was in first grade. It is a blue, leather-bound King James version with my name embossed on the cover in silver lettering. I still treasure it. It is worn by years of church-toting, reading, and underlining. There are notes in the margins, little scraps of bulletins and devotional notes and quotes littering its pages. I treasure this gift—which came with an almost magical aura of power. As a first-grader I had *my own BIBLE!* There was an emboldening power of possessing the Word of God, and the implication was that I, as a first-grader, had all the tools I needed to read and fully understand this magnificent book. Many people believe that. I do not. The Bible is wonderful, but it is also terrible. It is comforting, but it is also frightening. The Bible has the power to change hearts, but it has threatened lives and the course of nations.

We demand driver training and gun safety and require that our teachers have the right diplomas and educational certificates, but for the Bible, a tool that is as powerful as any gun ("the pen is mightier than the sword"), a tool that has as much potential for unlocking the future of children of all ages, we just say, "Here it is! Have at it!"

If you're at least as smart as a first-grader, you can read the Bible. If we value the Bible as we claim, we need to think again.

Several years ago I had a vision for some blog entries. I sometimes get accused of being long-winded (not always unfairly). I imagined a prescription for blog entries that would address Christian themes from my progressive Christian bent. Here's how I described it in my introductory post:

> My idea is simple: Take a one-word subject (Jesus, Bible, Sin, Salvation, etc.), and tease out my current understanding in a page or less. It's like the elevator speech I dread having to give (and so far haven't even managed to produce). But now is the chance—one subject, condensed into one page, single spaced, 12-point font, 1-inch margins. With a title on the page, you can put about 675 words in that space, so that will be the limit. I'm not going to do research (except the quotes and references that are running around in my crowded little brain). It'll just be me, in one page or less. A.Page.Or.Less. What I believe. With no A.P.O.L.ogy. ("Apologetics" is the discipline of defending one's beliefs.)

I only wrote one entry. I didn't get much response, and my interests turned elsewhere, but the first entry was on the Bible—because that is where it all begins. This is so even for many who don't "believe" in the Bible, because in one way or another, the changes our culture is experiencing are being framed by the Bible. Those from a secular or liberal perspective who argue that these issues are not about the Bible are inadvertently playing into the hands of, proving the point of the literalists who claim that this is exactly what the Bible says they will say! All the controversial issues are framed, left and right, between the "biblical position" and some alternate, non-biblical leftist position (which leaves us left-of-center Bible lovers in something of a dither). Here's that original post:

The Bible: With No A.P.O.L.ogy

It starts here, there is no doubt, because my beliefs are often met with dismay and the inevitable and apoplectic response, "How could you believe that? The Bible says…"

These may be the most common words of justification or explanation (and condemnation) in our society, because even though we are running headlong into a blind date with secularism, the Bible still has a hold on us. Western culture is so saturated in biblical imagery and language that what "the Bible says" becomes a kind of gospel, even for many who don't believe in the Gospel—it's just in the air we breathe. So, "the Bible says" becomes a cultural vetting (even though many don't know if "A penny saved is a penny earned" is Bible or Ben Franklin). For believers, Conservative fundamentalists frame the world on the literal Word of God (essentially, the words of God), and liberal fundamentalists are just as challenged, rejecting far more than is necessary because education and experience won't let them accept literalism. (And they weren't listening in class to hear there is another way to read!) So, the extremes frame the argument around a literal Bible.

And that's the problem.

The British scholar C. H. Dodd once said there is no such thing as an intelligent "literal reading of the Bible." Everything is heard and interpreted subjectively. How could it be possible to get my own experience completely out of the way and truly hear objectively? (It is not.)

So we begin here because, yes, I know what the Bible says…about women and homosexuals and *the way, the truth, the life* (John 14). But I also know what it says about tattoos and rebellious children and women wearing jewelry. So, given my education and experience, here's my rather simple perspective:

There Is Another Way to Read the Bible.

A "black and white" literalism diminishes the Bible's message. Nothing is in the Bible because it is historically reliable, chronologically essential, or scientifically verifiable. "The point" of the text is always deeper than its surface value. Always. The creation narrative isn't about how long it took God to speak a universe into being. Jonah isn't about an historical man and a very large ichthyoid. Biblical "history" is not eyewitness newspaper reporting, and those church rules can't just be transferred across millennia, miles, and cultures without some interpretation. And resurrection isn't just about something that happened to the body of a first-century Jewish martyr (it happens to you, too!). The Bible has been called "Salvation History." Like most good writing it was never meant to be literal history, only. Biblical truth is more poetry than prose, seeking to communicate God's work in this world through words, which always get in the way of the experience. And God's work itself is not "literal," but spiritual. It can only be seen by faith. We cannot "prove" God's work—or disprove the skeptic's alternate vision—so biblical narrative is a testimony, not a proof, it is descriptive, not prescriptive, it is prepositional, not propositional. As such, biblical narratives are sometimes "less" than factual—but they are always more than (and more important than) "just the facts, ma'am."[3]

Science is not in conflict with the Bible, and our reading must reflect current scientific understandings. Collective human experience (not just what seems right to me) is an important means of interpreting an ancient text. Biblical scholarship can provide nuanced understandings of texts two or three millennia after their composition. We must listen to all of this wisdom as we read. This is how God speaks. Doing so will continue to change the way we understand what "the Bible says." But that will be nothing new. Just ask Peter, who stood on that rooftop in Joppa one day, and after God opened his eyes to a completely different way to read his Bible, he said, "Now I understand" (Acts 10).

May it be so!

There *is* another way to read the Bible.

I love the Bible. The litanies and prayers I write for worship are filled with biblical references. My sermons are chock full of allusions and direct quotations. I memorized a lot of scripture as a young person, so it just comes out in my preaching and teaching (you know the measure of a good preacher is the number of Bible verses he can quote in one sermon!). There is no greater literary treasure for Western civilization and no greater repository of spiritual testimony and poetry and wisdom in the world—but our obsession with the literal "Word of God" is failing us, and such literalism is failing the Bible.

The sin of "bibliolatry" is insidious and always threatens to replace the worship of God, as all idols do. Some fundamentalists may actually "believe in the Bible" more than they believe in God. The American South is littered with "Bible churches," and as important as the Bible is, there is something fundamentally misplaced about that description. These are not "God churches" or "following-Jesus churches" or "changing the neighborhood churches." "Bible-believing" churches, another commonly used descriptor, really just means "Bible believing—if you believe it like we believe it." The emphasis requires conforming to certain literalisms of biblical interpretation instead of approaching the mystery of God with an openness to let the spirit *move where it wills* (John 3:8).

We need to learn to read again. There is another way to read the Bible—and it's a better way. It's better for the Bible and better for us. Let me unpack a few words from my own "apologetic":

The Bible has been called 'Salvation History.' Like most good writing it was never meant to be literal history, only…. Biblical narrative is a testimony, not a proof, it is descriptive, not prescriptive, it is prepositional, not propositional."

A helpful place to begin is to understand that the Bible is not, strictly speaking, "history." Scholars understand that many of the dates and chronologies in the Bible are inaccurate. This doesn't mean the Bible is wrong; it just means dates aren't of primary importance—because they were not necessarily important to the writer. Something much more significant is at stake. What is at stake is "salvation history." While a good history is dependent on correct dates and times, facts and figures, the truth of salvation history could hardly care less.

I can still feel those warm waters. I still know the aura of that room, can feel the Holy pulsing through my racing heart. I can still hear my daddy's voice as he stood in those waters of blessing with me: "In obedience to the divine command of our Lord and Savior, Jesus Christ, and upon your profession of faith in him, I baptize you now, my son." For my life, and for my faith, that day will always be significant. It marked a beginning—though there was never a day in my life that I can remember not being a "Christian." Such is the power of religious ritual. There is no magic in the water, no "hocus pocus" in the air. No door to heaven opened that day because I jumped through the right legalistic hoop, said the right prayer in the right place, accompanied that prayer with the right amount of water—but that experience, that very tangible expression of an internal conviction and hope, changed my relationship to God. I will never forget it.

I have no idea if it was November or July, and it was around 1976, but that date could be wrong by several years. Knowing the correct date, however—or not knowing it—does not change the experience in the slightest. The significance of my baptism is not my history; it is my "salvation history"—my experience of God in this world. In the place and time of my childhood church, God spoke to me. One way I responded was to the call of an initiation of faith called baptism by immersion. As I look back on my life, though my theological understandings have changed immensely from what I knew (or thought I knew as a twelve-year-old boy), nothing has changed about the significance of that experience. I probably could not prove to you that it happened. Maybe there's a record in a filing cabinet at that First Baptist Church, maybe a church bulletin in my mother's scrapbook, a keepsake, maybe not. I don't need to prove it to you. It's my experience. All that needs to be true about it is true, regardless of the provable facts.

That is just as it is with the Bible.

It does not matter when old Abram marched out of the land of Ur to a destination God promised to show him—or even if Abram was an actual, historical figure or not (and many biblical scholars, Christian and Jewish, think he was not). It does not matter when King David heralded the unified monarchy of ancient Israel—or even if there is enough evidence to justify a claim to any significant "house of David" in Israel around 1000 B.C.E. (and many archaeologists say there is not). It does not matter that the "exodus" from Egypt—as a single historical event involving the transmigration of several hundred thousand people en masse—is disputed by most reputable scholars.

I *do* understand that because of the way many people were taught to understand the Bible, "disproving" such central, biblical events would discredit the Bible and would be a powerful evidence for disproving faith. "Either it's all true or none of it is true," they say. Such a claim, however, sadly misses the point. It *is all true*—in the way spiritual truth is reckoned. God's work is never dependent upon, defined by, or limited to "just the facts." The point of "Bible believing" is proving that the Bible is "true"—you do not really need faith; you just have to "believe the Bible." But this is actually an interesting contradiction of the definition of faith: "*the assurance of things hoped for* [not proven], *the conviction of things not seen*" (Heb 11:1).

God calls us. And our willingness to respond, to step out in faith, to go "*to the land that I will show you*" (Gen 12:1) is still the sum and substance of faith (Abraham's story). God's work is always the unlikely, improbable, unthinkable task of calling light out of darkness (the creation story), giving life where there is no life (resurrection), installing shepherds as kings and establishing everlasting kingdoms in earthly places (King David's story). God's call is freedom, the unbinding of the powers, the journey of liberation, and it almost always involves spending some time in the wilderness (the exodus).

It is all true.

Does this mean there is no basis in history to the biblical narrative? On the contrary, what gives the Bible its poignancy, its power, is that the stories of creation and exodus and resurrection are all told by real people. These narratives capture the actual experience of life and liberation and redemption experienced in reality. The fact that there are apparent contradictions in the "facts" of the stories only serves as evidence of this reality. Ask three eyewitnesses the details of a crime, and you will likely get divergent "facts."

The Bible has been called 'Salvation History.' Like most good writing it was never meant to be literal history, only.

There are always multiple layers of stories told in order to advance spiritual truth. Events of the story may or may not be, strictly speaking, "historical," but the point is not to argue "the facts." The point is to understand the experience that lies behind the telling of the story. The writer Robert Fulghum understands this truth when he says, "Imagination is stronger than knowledge—myth is more potent than history—dreams are more powerful than facts—hope always triumphs over experience—laughter is the cure for grief—love is stronger than death."[4]

Biblical narrative is a testimony, not a proof, it is descriptive, not prescriptive, it is prepositional, not propositional.

A testimony is the most personal truth, the most important truth that can be told. The Bible should never be reduced to a "proof" of anything. It is so much more important than that. The stories are descriptive—they describe the situations and experiences of people, just like you and me, in their encounter with God. Those experiences are not supposed to exactly *prescribe* the only experience and the only response to the experience of God. That experience will always be personal, individual, contextual.

Biblical truth is "prepositional," by which I mean it is about experience. A grammatical preposition describes relationship (on, to, under, at, about, of) as biblical stories describe the relationship of people to one another—and those people to God, as they understood God at the time. To reduce biblical narratives to "propositions" is to remove them from the living, relational experience of those people. The Bible knows this and reminds us, "*the letter kills, but the Spirit gives life*" (2 Cor 3:6). Insisting the Bible is "the letter of the law" is to misunderstand the essential character of a text of witness, testimony, poetry. As we read the experiences of those recorded in the Bible and relate to them (or not), our own faith is informed and deepens within us. That is the power of story; it resonates with Spirit.

About fifteen years ago I was invited to bring my guitar to our children's camp and to lead the music. I asked what kind of music I should prepare and inquired about a theme song. When I learned that there was no theme song, I decided to try to write one. It was my first musical composition, and for all the years since, I have written one song a year, whether I had anything to say or not! I cannot imagine the thrill of being a world-class entertainer, because hearing 150 kids sing my music at the top of their lungs one week each year is about all the affirmation and adoration I can take!

A few years ago my song was about the biblical story, and we sang the chorus this way:

That's my story that I have told
(I've told so you could know)
All that's true for me is a truth that's been told.
I have lived the story, no facts to be sold.
That's my story—a tale of glory—that's my story
and I'm stickin' with it![5]

The narrative of the song suggests that "my story" may be as farcical as the old excuse about the dog eating your homework or as ridiculous as the man who claimed no responsibility for his house fire because his bed "was on fire when I lay down on it!"[6] Or my story may be as audacious as the one that claims, "I once was lost but now am found, was blind but now I see."[7] The song ends, as does a proper understanding of the Bible: The proof is in the truth of love lived better. That's my story, and I'm sticking with it.

We need to learn to read again. Making the Bible into a simple "rulebook" makes it into a cold, static, often-condemning word that in many ways is outdated. It allows us to turn the Bible into a weapon, a bludgeon, a tool for justifying our own prejudices, our own preconceived truths. Such a view of Scripture denies the rich depth of its poetic and narrative quality, its inspired voice to convey a unique, transcendent Truth.

The American poet Wallace Stephens once noted,

The final belief is to believe in a fiction,
which you know to be a fiction, there
being nothing else. The exquisite truth
is to know that it is a fiction and that
you believe in it willingly.[8]

Do not misunderstand *fiction* to mean false. *Fiction* refers to a truth that is related to and told within a story. Good fiction always conveys a truth that is *more than fact*. Biblical truth invites us into a narrative, to find ourselves caught up in the fiction of God's story, a story that is being written for us, by us, in us, with us.

That day in Old Testament class, I was introduced to The Story, which has changed my life in a way that a literal Bible never could. Before that class I was only looking for proofs to confirm my preconceived ideas of what the Bible is (letting the Bible just prove the Bible). Through a new way of reading that is not restricted by facts and laws and rules and proof, I continue to find God, as I find my own story in The Story.

That proof is all the Truth I need.

That Truth is all the proof I need.

Listening Now for the Word of the Lord[9]

2 Kings 22:1–2, 8, 11–13; 23:1–3; 2 Timothy 3:14–16 and Hebrews 4:12

Russ Dean, July 24, 2005

Years ago I was asked a simple question: "Is the Bible the Word of God, or does the Bible contain the 'Word of God'?" I didn't know at the time that the question was not really so simple. It was really a trick question, a litmus test for a growing evangelical orthodoxy—at the center of which was not God, or Jesus who reveals God to us, but an argument over the "inerrancy of the scriptures."[10] It is the argument that divided the Southern Baptist Convention (at least on the surface) and continues its divisive work throughout denominations and around the globe as the church, embarrassingly, continues to wield the Bible as a sword. I was a youth when the question was asked, and though in my father's church we did not use a liturgical response to the reading of scripture, I knew the traditional refrain: "This is the Word of the Lord. Thanks be to God." I thought, "Well, we say, 'This *is* the Word of the Lord'" (not "The reading you have just heard might *contain* the Word of the Lord"), so I answered, orthodoxically correct (at least in the eyes of my inquisitor), "The Bible *is* the Word of God."

Today, I would answer her question differently.

What do our children learn from the words we say, often thoughtlessly, over and again ([hold up Bible] "*This* is the Word of the Lord. Thanks be to God)? By the simple labels we attach to people and things (*the Jews* said)? By the sweeping generalizations they hear (*Christians* believe)? What tenets of a "popular religion" have permeated even our subconsciousness so that we do not even realize their impact on our lives? Are all of these words, simply because they are found in a book that we call "the Bible," best understood by such an *absolute* description—"*the* Word of the Lord?" (Is every word herein equally "*the* Word"? Is there no other "Word of the Lord?")

I believe that we suffer an incalculable loss in that this diverse collection of sacred texts, written over a period of a thousand years or more, has come to be known too simply as "*the Bible.*" "The Bible" implies a simplicity, a unity, a directionality, an authority that belies the truth of the history of this collection and that betrays the life-giving inspiration that a true, "living Word" can bring.[11] In a conference on the authority of the Bible, Hugh Dawes reminded his hearers that the Greek phrase *ta biblia* means not "the Bible" but "the books" (plural).[12]

One of the great tragedies of contemporary Christianity is that we have reduced a few of the hints of the truth of God, experienced by a few of the people of God, to bite-sized nuggets of a too-easy moralism. If I had a nickel for every time someone said, "*The Bible* says," I'd be a rich man. Do you understand the weight of that simple statement? It implies that if we can simply attach the imprimatur, the official weight, of *the Bible* says to any statement (because it is "*the* Word of God"), then we can be free to rest easy in our action (or in our complacency), in our hospitality (or in our greed), in our acceptance (or in our condemnation)—the operative word being *our*. Saying *the Bible says* is really just a way of trying to justify ourselves—which is hardly the intent of any biblical passage.[13]

Our culture, too accustomed to having everything handed to us on that proverbial "silver platter," our culture of instant gratification and easy access and drive-through convenience and just-for-me comfort, has demanded a Scripture that is just that easy. And the church has unfortunately responded, boiling down a thousand years of ancient literature into a pabulum of easy aphorisms of *the Bible says* ("This is the Word of the Lord"). In doing so we've provided a proof-texting formula, which ironically (and contrary to the nature of Scripture) allows the Bible to be used as a guarantee of the rightness of *our own* prejudices. (When I gave our administrative assistant the text to use for today's bulletin cover, "The Bible in Fifty Words," which I intended somewhat tongue-in-cheek, she read it and then said, "Oh, that's cute!" I smiled at the irony. Exactly.)[14]

The Jewish and Christian scriptures, a library of wisdom (*ta biblia*), a collection of diverse and often contradictory opinions about God and God's work in our difficult world, have been transformed into a "sacred lite" in our world of convenience. Cute. Little. Truths. And too many preachers have come to see their vocation as simply that of telling their people what "the Bible says." Gregory Jones of Duke University is surely right that we have "flatten[ed] scripture [by reading] the text only for what lies behind it (that is, some nugget of historical "proof"), or in segments (such as, only the gospels are really important) or as a collection of guidelines for moral living."[15]

Why is it that we love to spend *hours* on the beach with Danielle Steele and John Grisham and that our kids are even turning off their X-Boxes and their jam boxes to devour at lightning speed J. K. Rowling's latest 650 pages of pure imagination—and all the while the church is trying its best to distill the greatest truth there is into some kind of just-tell-me-what-it-says "Top Ten List"?

In his lecture Hugh Dawes says that reading for such simplicity has not always been the case:

Only with the reformation did this change, the bible becoming both *the book* and most definitely also a *single* book, with the individual writings within it seen now as far less important than its unified function as a coherent guide to the christian (sic) life. As such it was most certainly authoritative…[supplying] rules, beliefs, laws and codes of conduct, which were enforceable, and to which the subjects of a Christian kingdom must submit themselves.[16]

We have at our disposal a treasured spiritual library filled with Harlequin romance and murder mystery, with geopolitical conflict and historical biography, a spiritual library of personal witness and devotional classics—and the church has largely diminished it to a moralistic set of rules: *The Bible* says do this. *The Bible* says don't do that. *This is the Word of the Lord.* Thanks be to God. We need to quit saying *the Bible says*, and we need to start reading Scripture more as the great literature that it is, listening more to its story, and letting it speak its truth *to us*.

I believe a word is not a "living word" *just* because it's in the Bible.[17] There are lots of words in the book, as you know, that we have to strain to make live. There are others, in fact, that I cannot make live except by using them as examples in the negative—in other words, to say, "What these people heard, and said, and did, as recorded in our book, is certainly *not* the Word of the Lord." (Thanks be to God!) And, conversely, there are many "living words" that come to us from other sources as well, whether literary, artistic, natural, or experiential. But the scriptures remain our best source as a church, I believe, a resource whose depths we have not begun to plumb in opening our eyes and our minds, our hearts and our ears, our hands and our lives to God's living Word.

At Furman Pastor's School a few weeks ago, Dr. Will Willimon, former dean of the chapel at Duke and now Bishop Willimon of the United Methodist Church, asked me if Rick Warren of Saddleback Church in California, famed author of *The Purpose Driven Life*, was one of my preaching models with his straightforward, "Here's what it says—now let me tell you what it means" style. I laughed out loud![18]

I'm sorry if you want me to hand you "the Word of the Lord" each week in three points and a poem. I just cannot do it. And I will not do it, because I do not believe this is possible. If you want the Word of God to be a true, life-giving Word, it's going to take a little work: *You* are going to have to listen to that ancient story as carefully as you can, and you are going to have to listen in every now ("now" in the anthem, "now" in the sermon, "now" in the fellowship that follows worship, "now" in the work and service, the joys and sorrows of busy lives[19]) to determine what in that grand story resonates with, and what in that ancient story is in conflict with, the story of your own life and the Truth you have discerned through your life. Only in finding *life* in these words, or any others, can it become "the Word of the Lord."

Walter Wink, of Auburn Theological Seminary, says, "We can no longer simply submit to scripture without asking whether new light is needed to interpret it. I for one do not abandon scripture, but neither do I acquiesce. I wrestle with it. I challenge it. I am broken and wounded by it, and in that defeat I sometimes encounter the living God."[20]

I have not abandoned the Bible. It is more important to me than ever. But I will not simply call it "*the Word* of the Lord." For me there is an implied arrogance in such a claim, and the dangers of misunderstanding and misusing "the Word of God" for my own benefit are too great. History is replete with examples.

It is my continuing prayer for this congregation, however, that we will keep the old lamp (Ps 119:105) burning brightly. Its beautiful light will never be extinguished. But I also pray for the courage and the conviction to look *always* for new light as well, from whatever source we may find it, that in the ancient story, made ever new, we may even encounter "the Word of the Lord."

Because it will always change our lives when we do so: Let us listen now for the Word of the Lord.

May it be so!

Notes

[1] Stanley Hauerwas, *Unleashing the Scripture: Freeing the Bible from Captivity to America*, (Nashville, TN: Abingdon Press, 1993), 15.

[2] Ibid, 15.

[3] These are signature words from detective Joe Friday, the main character in the old television show *Dragnet*.

[4] Robert Fulghum, *All I Really Need to Know I Learned in Kindergarten* (New York: Ballantine Books, 2004).

[5] Russ Dean, "That's My Story," 2016.

[6] The title of the book, *It Was on Fire When I Lay Down On It*, by Robert Fulghum, is derived from a story he tells. A firefighter responding to a call found a house with a bed on fire. The firefighter questioned the tenant about how the fire started, and the man responded, "I don't know. It was on fire when I lay down on it."

[7] This line is from the text of the hymn, a perennial favorite, "Amazing Grace" (John Newton, 1779): "Amazing Grace, how sweet the sound, that saved a wretch like me. I once was lost, but now am found, was blind but now I see."

[8] Wallace Stevens, *Opus Posthumous: Poems, Plays, Prose* (New York: Random House, 2011), 189.

[9] Our Advent theme in 2002 was "God, the Good Ole' Days, and the Story of Christmas." Due to some theological questions I had been having about the traditional, liturgical response to the reading of Scripture ("This is the Word of the Lord. Thanks be to God.") and in keeping with the theme for this series, we changed our response to, "You have heard the ancient STORY. Let us listen now for the Word of the Lord." This has been our response ever since, and on a number of occasions, people have expressed their disapproval or frustration at this non-traditional usage. Today's sermon is in response to another question concerning this response.

[10] I have said more recently, as I have come to more fully understand the issue at the heart of this question, that it seems to me that fundamentalist Christians believe in the Bible more than they believe in God. I have great love for the Bible, but it is not God and should not be treated as if it were, of itself, "divine."

[11] Perhaps more importantly, when "the Bible" becomes so small and manageable, we insulate ourselves from the "two-edged" nature of the indictments of a "living word." A manageable Bible is used as a weapon against others, whereas the true nature of Scripture is to be a word, "living and active, sharper than any two-edged sword" [cutting both ways] (Heb 4:12).

[12] Hugh Dawes, "By Whose Authority?" *ProgressiveChristianity.org*, April 2006, https://progressivechristianity.org/resources/by-whose-authority/.

[13] At this point I ventured from my manuscript and, in an apparently impassioned tone (according to later reports by my wife!), asked our congregation to "Please quit saying THE BIBLE SAYS…"

[14] I cannot find an author for this little poem, though it is easy to find on the internet: "God made, Adam bit, Noah arked, Abraham split, Joseph ruled, Jacob fooled, bush talked, Moses balked, Pharaoh plagued, people walked, sea divided, tablets guided, promise landed, Saul freaked, David peeked, prophets warned, Jesus born, God walked, love talked, anger crucified, hope died, Love rose, Spirit flamed, Word spread, God remained."

[15] Gregory Jones, "Imagining Scripture," *The Christian Century*, (June 19–26, 2002). The entire quotation, which was placed in our order of service for today is: "It seems to me a wonderful irony that Christians in America are preoccupied with debates about biblical authority just when all parties to the debates are less knowledgeable about the content of scripture than many of our predecessors were…. Could it be that know less of the content of scripture because we have made it so boring? We flatten scripture when we read the text only for what lies behind it, or in segments or as a collection of guidelines for moral living. Who wouldn't rather read *Beloved* than study a series of texts that we cannot connect to a larger narrative, much less to our convictions about the Triune God whom we worship?"

[16] Hugh Dawes, "By Whose Authority?" *ProgressiveChristianity.org*, April 2006, https://progressivechristianity.org/resources/by-whose-authority/.

[17] This is the answer I now give to the sermon's opening question. As I was considering hymns for today's service with our minister of music, the only hymn I could recall from memory was "Holy Bible, Book Divine." Is it surprising, then, that as a youth I would have answered as I did? Don't we, in fact, learn most of our theology from the hymns we commit to memory?

[18] I had just preached on evolution ("t=0 and Counting: Lessons Along this Darkened Path") and on the problem of evil and my conviction that we should learn to say that God is not "all powerful" ("Grasping at Silk: Everlasting Arms and the Problem of Pain"). My preaching, and this may rightly be a critique, is anything but Warren-esque!

[19] At some point we added to our bulletin a footnote concerning our scriptural response: "The challenge an ancient text presents to modern readers is to allow the truth that originally animated the text to become a 'living Word' for us. Only as we interact with a given text in a continual 'now' ('now' in the anthem, 'now' in the sermon, 'now' in the fellowship that follows worship, 'now' in the work and service, the joys and sorrows of busy live) can that Word truly become *living and active* (Heb 4:12)."

[20] The quotation ends, "I will not concede the field, therefore, to a putative orthodoxy that dodges the hermeneutical task." A Reply by Walter Wink: A conversation on gays and the Bible," August 14, 2002, https://www.christiancentury.org/article/2002-08/reply-walter-wink.

A New Future:
Too Many Christians Aren't Ready to Live

Questions to Consider

What do you believe about heaven? Hell?

Are heaven and hell actual, physical places? Is there any other way to understand these concepts?

How important is the afterlife (understanding it, preparing for it) to your faith?

What is the "soul"? Is this an actual, literal thing, an essence that exists inside the "container" of your body?

What is "salvation"? Is salvation a transaction or a process? Is it for a person or for a people (i.e., is it individualistic or communal/social)?

Is Christianity's understanding of soul and salvation primarily concerned with the here-and-now or the afterlife?

What would be the change in your practice of faith, today, if "soul" and "salvation" were concepts rooted in the here-and-now?

❖

Doesn't everything die at last, and too soon?
Tell me, what is it you plan to do
with your one wild and precious life?
"Tell Me…,"
—Mary Oliver[1]

The Christian view of life always excited me. As I learned it as a child, we are part of a larger-than-(this)-life drama. We are bit actors. God is the producer and director. Jesus is the hero. The plot is simple, but, like all good dramas, it contains a twist: Nice people live ordinary lives, sometimes boring, sometimes exciting, and as we walk our way through our *threescore years and ten* (as you quote Ps 90:10, cue the ominous music!), we are walking, every one of us, mindlessly, invariably, helplessly…to our deaths. Because that is the life we have been given. We are cursed from the beginning. We Baptists didn't believe in "original sin" like the Catholics taught, but we did believe Eve's appetite and Adam's weakness have marked us all, and without some help, some serious intervention, all are destined for the grave. And worse.

Hell awaits.

But God has made a way. After making it impossible (not virtually impossible, but actually, literally impossible) to affect our own healing, to find our way or work our way or plead our way out of the great abyss that is our fated destination, God has given us a way out. That way (the only way) is through a sacrifice made to satisfy God's great honor, God's untouched holiness—which has been touched and broken and stained by our inevitable, helpless dishonor. Even to redeem ordinary people, according to this grand narrative, no ordinary sacrifice would do. A perfect sacrifice will be needed, an unblemished sacrifice, a spotless lamb.

Abraham's story is worth remembering here. His fate was sealed because his barren wife, Sarah, had left him childless, but through a miracle of divine intervention, that old, dried up womb became fecund with life, and a child (named "Laughter") was born. Isaac was the future—the only future Abraham and Sarah had. He was their life, their hope—until God called Abraham to take that life, put a knife into it, and let that hope pour out on an altar of obedience. Wow. What a story. And it is the Christian faith story too—except that, unlike Abraham's story of obedience, no ram was to be found in the thicket to save Jesus. God had made Jesus, born in perfect sinlessness, the incarnate Son of God, to be the perfect sacrifice, and his lifeblood, given on our sorry, helpless behalf, is our only salvation.

This is the story of the countless evangelical sermons that punctuated my formative mind, my impressionable emotions as a child. I was part of a larger-than-(this)-life drama. God, reaching down from beyond space and time, has made a way for me personally. Jesus is the way. He died to pay the penalty, to be the sacrifice, for me.

The story was real and heart-rending. It was the ending of a thousand teary "let's sing one more stanza" altar calls for repentance, the movement toward life-changing decision in all the emphatically revivalist worship services I have attended in my life. When any of those services ended with someone walking the aisle, giving their life to Jesus, accepting in their heart that he died for them too, heaven quaked, the angels sang, and we were there to witness it. It was as if the entire universe stopped. The veil of time was torn for just a moment as the realm of this war-weary, sin-sick, suffering-laden world was bathed in the light of heavenly joy.

I cannot adequately convey the magnitude of this feeling, knowing that this grand, eternal plan was being affected right before my eyes. Salvation had come, in a moment, and from that moment on, for all eternity (it was mostly for eternity), a soul had been saved from God's wrath (which we all deserve, being hopelessly sinful and helplessly lost), and from that moment on, heaven awaited. That's what it's all about. This life is just a trial, a test, a theatrical prequel to the real thing, the only thing.

It's about heaven. Getting to heaven.

All of here is just about there. All of now is just about then. All of this is just about that. All earthly pain and joy is almost illusory; it doesn't really count. All joys will be so overshadowed that they hardly deserve to be called joys. All suffering will be so redeemed that it doesn't really matter; maybe we shouldn't worry about it at all—our suffering or theirs (the poor, the sick, the hungry children). This isn't what it's about. Their suffering will end, if they accept Jesus, and it will all be worthwhile. Looking back (but who will look back?), it will just be a minor, unnoticeable blip on the cosmic scale of God's vision and plan.

Faith is about this future. As a minister told me once, "That's what it's all about. It doesn't matter how we get 'em in…just so we get 'em in!"

The present doesn't count; it's all about the future.

I do not intend to demean this story or those who taught it to me. The evangelical impulse is based in gratitude, a recognition that despite our childish retorts to the contrary, I really *cannot* "do it myself." A life lived from a foundation of gratitude and a necessary and healthy interdependence is a good life indeed. And the revivalistic imperative to "make a decision," to take a realistic look, an honest appraisal of one's own life, and to step forward—before God and everyone—and pronounce the intent to make a change, well, we could use more of that honest vulnerability and that intentionality as well.

I have just come to believe that as a cosmic drama, this story is hardly cosmic enough. It sounds all too similar to run-of-the-mill human "justice" than anything truly otherworldly. In this story God is little different from a very human sheriff, meting out a measured and equivalent punishment for wrongdoing and reward for merit. Where is the decisively different, divine-not-human grace and mercy and love in that kind of judgment? I thought God was the Great Mystery, the author of an altogether different system of justice?

Now is not the place to fully unpack this atonement theology, but suffice it to say the story claims to be based on the grace of a God of unconditional love, who offers a salvation of grace, not works—but that is not how it is most often conveyed. That "free" salvation saves us from the wrath of an all-powerful, jealous, and angry God who demands justification (where is the grace and unconditional love in that?). This just sounds more like a reworking of the age-old penalty-and-reward system. It's tit-for-tat justification: "Do the crime; serve the time." Jesus's innocent life becomes the payment to satisfy a bloodthirsty God. The way I grew up understanding it, God's love was not really unconditional at all (there was an ultimate *condition* required for my salvation), and the salvation wasn't based on grace, but on the demand that someone pay. (*Grace* is defined as "unmerited favor," but in this story our salvation isn't unmerited at all. It is merited—and with a very high price, the price of death.) Salvation was most definitely "earned" (it could hardly have been more costly), not freely given.

I have witnessed human beings offer unconditional love, undeserved forgiveness, the mercy of true grace. I have seen parents go far beyond any justice expected of them, crossing all reasonable lines of reward and punishment, to twist and bend and persist and persist and persist in loving a wayward child—never, ever giving up on her or him (whether or not the child ever "came home"). In those examples I find a hint of the true grace and unconditional love that I believe the Christian story is supposed to offer. We can find that grace in the life and story of Jesus, but only if we can learn to shuck the husks of a more familiar, and very earthly understanding of, justice.

The lesson I learned in this milepost along my life's winding journey was not about atonement theology. It was about what theologians call eschatology, the study of "last things." The Christian story as I learned it was finally an eschatological story, and it offered such a strongly emphasized future tense that there was no present that really counted for much of anything.

The powerful Robert Duvall movie called *The Apostle* opens with a scene that makes this clear. Duvall plays a Southern, evangelical preacher named Euliss F. "Sonny" Dewey. Deeply flawed, Dewey is a complex character driven by his passions—passion for the gospel and for women and strong drink and money and power. In the opening scene the preacher is driving on one of the country roads in his county when he comes upon the scene of a one-car accident. Obviously running at a high rate of speed, the wrecked car had run off the road, the driver unable to hold the curve. Down a slight embankment the car had overturned, leaving its badly damaged driver hanging upside down, his life hanging in the balance. "The Apostle" sees an opportunity to save the day, and he seizes it.

Grabbing his well-worn Bible, the preacher runs across the field and finds the driver only semiconscious but alert enough to hear an offer of soul-saving salvation. When the driver nods his head, moans his affirmation, Dewey whispers a prayer—and then he runs back to his car and drives off, apparently content to leave the man to die from his wounds, because, according to the narrative of my childhood faith, Dewey had done what was most needed. He saved the man—not by saving his life for today, but by offering a narrative that would save his soul for tomorrow. Whatever happened to his body was really of little concern.

It's all about the future.

There are few evangelicals so coolly distanced from human suffering and tragedy, but the theology I learned as a child made it clear that the future was, ultimately, all that counted. While faith *should* prompt us to love God by *loving our neighbors as ourselves* (Matt 22:39), the purpose of faith is not *this*-worldly. The question was, "If you died tonight, would you wake up in heaven?" not "If you wake up tomorrow, will you help those whose life is a living hell?"

My early faith was based in this kind of escapist framework. The world will not be transformed by our hands and feet, our hearts of compassion. On the contrary, our only hope will come from an otherworldly intervention, ultimately taking the form of the fiery, apocalyptic destruction of the earth and its inhabitants. Only those who find their salvation before it's too late will know God's kingdom. It will not be a kingdom come *"on earth as it is in heaven"* (Matt 6:10), for which Jesus taught his disciples to pray, but a kingdom come when earth has been destroyed and heaven and hell are all that remain.

That mindset will work on you subtly. Yes, we *need* to feed hungry children—but even if we can't feed them, or just don't feed them, we can save their souls. If they stay hungry now, even die of starvation, well, in the long run that's hardly anything to trifle over, so great will be their heavenly reward. Yes, the love of *Christ should* compel *us* (2 Cor 5:14) to live lives of compassionate action—but if we're too busy at the office or the club, well, we can send money to Africa and trust our missionaries to save souls. The end is all that matters, and it justifies the means. Yes, we *should* be concerned about inner-city poverty and the violence and the crime that results, but this life is only temporary, and in the grand, big picture, and the eternity of God's time, the suffering in this life will only last for the blink of an eye.

Whether evangelical Christians are aware of it or not, in this faith-future emphasis there is a powerful pull to the status quo: Even if we don't change any earthly woes, well, that's not really what matters anyway. There is a strong, implied justification for inaction, if not outright apathy: I *should* work, but even if I fail in this world, as long as I have trusted Jesus, I'll get my reward anyway. And so will they who suffer—I really needn't worry about suffering or despair.

As a college sophomore I could not have spoken any of this critique of my religious training. I certainly knew none of its cynicism. But in a very important way that changed one night, fairly dramatically. Appropriately, for the boy schooled in revivalism and impassioned by the evangelical fervor of the present moment (that decision that makes all things right for the eternal future), I learned one of the lessons that most dramatically altered my life…in a revival!

I was a sophomore at Furman and was in school there with my sister, a junior, and my brother, a freshman. As a child I had learned that every fall my father would be away for one week, participating in a revival in some Southern Baptist church along the eastern seaboard. Every Baptist church had a fall revival. Originally, many were two-week affairs, but by my childhood most churches had whittled down the intensity to a Sunday-through-Friday series of evening services. It was most common for pastors to invite a guest preacher and sometimes a musician. Together, these itinerant messengers would enlighten a congregation, appeal for a renewal of spirit and devotion, and, to a greater or lesser degree, depending on the flavor of the inviting pastor, appeal in a Friday-night altar call for congregants to make that all-important, eternity-altering decision for salvation.

Again, I intend no disrespect. There is nothing wrong with an appeal to renewal. We all need it from time to time. The American church perhaps needs a "revival" today as much as ever before. But the revivalism of this practice often leaned too heavily on emotionalism and guilt and focused too much on the ego of the evangelist and the numbers of converts and decisions—as if heaven kept a tally that directly accrued to the account of the soul-saver. Most progressive churches have let the annual revival fade into the history books, as has the First Baptist Church of Clemson, South Carolina—but not before a revival there in 1984 changed my life!

My father has always highlighted his pastoral and preaching ministry with his ability as a powerful baritone soloist. Not infrequently, his sermons would break into song, and he also honed his craft as a featured soloist for civic clubs and social organizations. In these annual revivals he was as often as not the guest musician, not the preacher, and in 1984 his singing had been paired with the preaching of Dr. Ken Chafin, a well-known Southern Baptist pastor from Louisville, Kentucky. (Dr. Chafin would later become my preaching professor at the Southern Baptist Seminary in Louisville.)

As was his habit, as often as possible my dad would invite his children to join him on stage. My sister is an amazing pianist, and my brother has a world-class tenor voice. I am an also-ran vocalist, so I often showed up with my trumpet in tow. On a Thursday night the three Dean siblings piled into my sister's blue Volkswagen beetle and made the thirty-minute drive from Greenville, South Carolina, through Easley and into that foothill Tiger Town, known as "Klimpsen" to all self-respecting South Carolinians. I don't remember what we sang, though I'm sure it was part of our standard repertoire, and I only remember one thing Dr. Chafin said…but it was all I needed to hear, probably all I had the capacity to hear that night.

The sermon text was John 10:10, a verse that has ever since been my favorite scripture: *I came that [you] may have life, and have it abundantly.* The text has no doubt found its home in many revivals, but probably not as Dr. Chafin emphasized it. I can imagine the impassioned plea of many evangelists, connecting "abundant" life with "eternal life," and pitching that text into a future-tense proclamation: "Jesus came so that when you die, you'll have eternal life (which is abundant!)."

But that's not what the text says, and Dr. Chafin made the point with a fine focus: "Too many Christians are ready to die who aren't ready to live yet."

In that moment I knew that he really was talking to me. Suddenly it became clear: What I've believed it's about is not really what it's about. I didn't give up my belief in an afterlife that night. I still haven't. I just realized that the focus of Jesus's life and ministry and teaching and his faith was almost completely focused in the here and now: *Thy kingdom come ON EARTH'* (Matt 6:10).

Love wildly.

Forgive daringly.

Fight for justice.

Breed compassion.

Teach equality.

Live today.

Trust tomorrow.

That one sermon changed my life. Almost in a moment everything shifted from future tense to present tense, from heaven to earth, from tomorrow to today, from there to here, from then to now. Dr. Chafin did use the words *eternal life*, but explained that there is no reason to equate eternal life as "after life." Eternal life begins now. It is fullness of life, abundance of living. It is possible now.

In that moment I glimpsed a new future—it is the future that is with us even now. All the potential that God holds for us in any tomorrow is with us (in potential) today. All of it. What God intends is not some escapist hope—the view that at some undetermined point in the future, life as God has designed it will begin, in some other place, in some other realm or reality. God intends us to know life to the full and to experience it now.

With the glimpse of a new future, my understanding of the present also changed. *This* is it. What God has in mind, all God has in store, we're living that potential now—so there is no treatment of people and issues as if we are dealing only with an intermediate response. (Life isn't just a trial run for the real thing.) Salvation is to be experienced now. The biblical word is *salve*[2]—to heal, to make complete or whole, to make well. So our work with people, their actual lives and their physical bodies, is of eternal importance. We cannot be concerned with people's souls and ignore their bodies. In fact, there is no way to separate the two.

The escapist nature of that old theology was also dependent on an escapist view of the nature of reality, which encompasses our understanding of the physical body. Many of us were raised, ironically, with a Gnostic view of the world, not a biblical one. In that dualistic view the body is corrupt while the "real" self is incorruptible and totally other than the flesh. In this dualism the body is contrary to, and opposed to, the soul. The former is bad; the latter is good. The former is false; the latter is true. This dualism of flesh versus spirit/soul has crept into the theological understanding of many Christians—though it is contrary to biblical thought.

In the creation narrative of Genesis 2, far from disdaining the physical as corrupt and evil, God stoops to use the dirt of the earth to form the human being, and God does not treat this very earthly body as just an outer vessel containing the "real essence" of the man (a fleshly holder for the soul within).

God breathed the breath of life in the man, *and he became* a living soul (Gen 2:7).

We do not *have* souls—we *are* souls. We are living, embodied souls.

Trained in this Hebraic world of thought, Paul's understanding of the importance and unity of the body is made clear in his discussion of resurrection. There is a physical body and a spiritual body—but there is *no* life without a *body*. There is no disembodied "soul" inside the body. All human life is *embodied!* According to Paul's detailed description in 1 Corinthians 15, when we die, the soul does not rise up out of the body, only that ghostly apparition to live immortally. On the contrary, when the physical body dies, just as a seed is planted in the ground, another new and different *body* rises to new life. While it may be convenient to think of Paul's "spiritual body" the same way, many conceive of a disembodied human soul, the two concepts are not to be mistaken.

An eternal soul, separate and distinct from the physical body, is dependent upon a dualistic nature of reality (the body versus the soul, physical versus spiritual). Nurturing this soul would require escaping from the body, either through spiritual or mental enlightenment, which has been the practice of various forms of Gnosticism over two millennia, or through the destruction of the physical body. The death of this physical form would allow for the final emancipation of the soul. In such a dualistic world it would be easy to disdain all things physical—to regard pain as illusory, temporary, suffering as just a symptom of the flesh (inconvenient, but of no real consequence). All attention would be placed on the soul and the life and the world to come.

This is not Paul's theology—nor is it consistent with the central Christian conviction of *incarnation*, which insists that God is known to us in the flesh, has been made incarnate, to know and participate in the physical nature of reality. Far from absconding from our physical reality, remaining distinct and separate in a "supernatural" or "spiritual" realm, the divine and human are enmeshed together.

My interest in Paul's resurrection theology is a direct result of glimpsing the new future Dr. Chafin gave me in that revival sermon—and my interest has little to do with afterlife theology. I don't know exactly what Paul meant by a "spiritual body," though I am convinced his concept was holistic, in keeping with Hebraic theology, not dualistic, as influenced by later Greek philosophy. My concern with his theology is not to use it to speculate about what kind of "body" we might actually inhabit in the next life.

My concern is what his concept implies for *this* life!

If we do not possess souls but are souls, and if bodies are important, in this life and the next, there can be no dualism in our preaching and teaching and mission and ministry. We must be concerned for the whole person. Salvation continues into the next life and world (whatever that may be)—but it begins here and now. Salvation concerns abundant living—for the whole person and for the whole community.

Salvation is physical—we cannot just be concerned about people's "souls." Salvation is corporate, communal, social—as social creatures we cannot separate "social justice" from "personal salvation." Salvation is a present-tense reality—because of the life and death and resurrection of Jesus, Christians should be ready to live and experience that fullness today!

Call or Sentence?
Why I Preach

Jeremiah 20:7–9; Mark 1:14–15

Russ Dean, April 2, 2005

I've known all my life that I was going to be a preacher. I have shared with you the little poem I wrote as a first-grader:

I want to be a preacher, I think it would be fun
To study every morning before the rising sun,
To stand up in the pulpit and preach before the crowd,
Then you think I wouldn't—oh, yes, I would be proud!

I remember my first "sermon." It was not uncommon for our parents to call us all, when we were children, to sing together, to read from my mother's King James Bible, and to end the day with sentence prayers. I was an excited young believer, eager to share, so I volunteered to lead the devotion one night. With the soul-saving excitement of a tent-revival evangelist, I entitled my first sermon, "Hurry Up, Before It's Too Late!" I was eager to preach and nervous when the time came, hoping for some response of affirmation or confirmation, of commendation or commitment. It all sounds so silly now (though my hopes have actually not changed to this day!), and I don't remember the response to that sermon, but to my knowledge, no one got saved there at the foot of my parents' bed!

I remember my father cautiously explaining to me that it was not enough to want to preach because he was a preacher. A *calling* to preach, he said, had to come from God. So I listened in that environment that fostered a sense of calling, and my gifts were recognized and encouraged by people who cared about me and whose integrity I trusted, and the call came. It's never been very far from me: I *want* to be a preacher! *There is something like a burning fire shut up in my bones.* It was true very early in my life; it still is today.

I've known all my life that I was *going* to be a preacher. It's been a lifelong calling, and for you to have given me an outlet for that *burning fire* within me is an answer to my prayers. But I can also relate to the weary prophet who cried, *O Lord, you have enticed me, and I was enticed; you have* overpowered *me, and you have prevailed.*[3] I *want* to be a preacher, to be sure, but the idea of a "call to ministry" was so deeply implanted in my brain as a unilateral decision (it was *God's* decision!) that I'm not sure I ever really gave a half-serious thought to anything else. As much as I love science, for example, I took only the one science course required at Furman for non-science majors. (You see, I was *going* to be a preacher—like it or not!)

The greatest curse of the pastorate is that the discovery of your vocation virtually guarantees an ending to any conversation you are holding in any secular setting—no matter how much you seem to have had in common with the other person to that point. Things rock along fine until you say, "Oh, I'm a minister. And what do you do?" I generally get to hear something like, "Yeah! My grandmother was a Baptist. Now, if you'll excuse me...." *For the world of the Lord has become for me a reproach and derision all day long.*

I want to be a preacher, to be sure. But I also just want to be me, and whatever it is that we associate with the vocation of the pastor, it obviously conflicts with many people's sense of regular old selfhood. So I can understand old Jeremiah, tired of becoming a *laughingstock all day long* because his chosen (or assigned) mission in life had made him misunderstood by so many for so long.

So I have learned to ask, only a little tongue-in-cheek(!), "Is it a *call* to preach that I'm answering? Or is it really a *life sentence?*"

I don't think that I'm alone in my feeling. Ministers almost universally view their vocation as "lonely work," but the thing that keeps *many* of us in the pulpit week after week is the pulpit itself. Who else in our society enjoys such a position? Call it privilege or opportunity, call it counsel or comfort, call it power or influence or a simple ego-driven need to hear your own voice. Call it what you will. It is amazing, in a fast-paced and driven world like ours that you give *anyone* twenty minutes of undivided attention every week. It is amazing, in a high-tech world such as ours, that you simply sit and listen. No gimmicks. No graphics. It is amazing, in a politically charged and polarized society, that week after week you come to hear one person offer his or her opinion on the world.

The Orthodox and Roman Catholic traditions view the Word of God as first and foremost conveyed in the sacraments. Pentecostals view the Word as most powerfully conveyed in charismatic acts of the Spirit. Between these two poles, Protestants have made a rather dramatic proclamation, namely, that the Word of God, the living Word, which inspires and transforms, is best conveyed in and through the spoken word. The sermon has always been at the heart of Protestant worship—too much so at times. This Lenten season we have sought to emphasize all of the aspects of our worship, each one in which we can "listen now for the Word of the Lord,"[4] each one, your staff believes, as important as the other. No one steps into a pulpit, though, without knowing that for many people the sermon is the reason for being here.[5] So let me make several brief observations about this important task.

First, I want to tell you that preaching is a high privilege. I don't need to tell you that preaching is emotionally laden for me, but perhaps I need to try to tell you why it is so, and that is simply because I find it continually awe-inspiring and humbling that you come, at least in some small measure, week after week, to hear what *I* have to say. Wow! Who am I to tell you what I think? Especially about God? And about people? And about God-with-people?[6] Without over-selling the role or overstating the task, it is clear to me that what is said from the pulpit is still important—that what I say does influence, at least to some degree, the way you think and act and behave. And who am I to offer such a word? I never step into this pulpit without being humbled by this privilege.

Second, I want to tell you that preaching is difficult. The well-known preacher and professor of homiletics Thomas Long says preaching is "a wild river, wide and deep."[7] As much as I love it, I don't mind telling you that it is also a great burden (I would have enjoyed our three days at the beach this week so much more if I had not had to return to write a sermon!). It is like writing a five-page research paper each time I stand here. What *can* I say, *again*, that will be well-informed, contemporary, informing, and challenging?[8] And, more importantly, how *do* I make subjects that I believe are of ultimate importance interesting and accessible to *such* a wide audience of listeners? Ernest T.

Campbell has rightly noted that "Sundays come toward the preacher like telephone poles by the window of a moving train." Can it really be time again?[9]

Not to play for your sympathy, I will tell you that I go away from it more days than not believing I have failed more than I have succeeded. Like two weeks ago when I preached down the street at Holy Comforter Episcopal Church and the woman said at the door, "That was hard. And that was dark. And I feel hopeless after listening to it!" (I wanted to say, "And how cheery is *take up your cross and follow me* really supposed to be?"[10]). And the comment that someone made to me just a few years ago: "I almost never understand a single thing you say." I have come to appreciate in five years of preaching that communicating in words is one of the greatest challenges human beings face. So preaching is, for me, joy and pain and serves as a microcosm of the world at large. How do we learn to talk to and hear from and understand one another?

Next, let me tell you that I believe in "the sermon" as an art form and as a means of communicating truth. Last night as we were returning from the beach, Amy was reading *Summer of the Monkeys* out loud in the truck. This is a wonderful story, and at the close of each chapter her mouth hardly shut before both boys urged, loudly, "Don't stop. Read some more. Momma, read another chapter!" When many preachers are turning to graphics and gimmicks, Powerpoint, videos and music, and fill-in-the blanks study guides distributed with their bulletins, I still believe there is power in the naked word, if it is spoken well.[11] And because English is such a rich language, I want the sermon to be an art form, using our language well, painting pictures with words, using similes and metaphors, utilizing poetry and prose.

I know that sometimes my sermons are too much, too dense, too difficult, but I have a hard time letting go of what one of my professors called a "high literary style," because I believe in the beauty of spoken language, and I simply refuse, perhaps at my own peril, to "dumb down" the sermon to three points and a poem and to preach self-help, or feel-good, or God-and-country theology—all of which are much too prevalent in pulpits today. I believe Scripture is filled with great truths, but I believe that Scripture and theology are difficult because they are about *life*, which is difficult. And I believe that dumbing down the sermon will not make your life any easier. It will only serve to make life and our faith in it more of an illusion than a reality.[12] So thank you for humoring me and for listening. Keep complaining if you need to. I promise you that I do not take this task lightly and that I struggle every week with how to communicate the good news, being true to my own deepest instincts, and aware of your very diverse needs as well.

Fourthly, I want to tell you why I believe in the power of the spoken word, and that is because I am a product of it. It was the spring of 1984. I was a sophomore at Furman and visiting my father, who was the guest musician for a revival at First Baptist Church in Clemson, South Carolina. The guest preacher was Ken Chafin, and his text was John 10:10: *I have come that you might have* life *and have it more abundantly.* The message was this: "Too many Christians," Dr. Chafin said, "are ready to die who aren't ready to live yet." I don't know what else he said, how he reinforced that idea, but I know that in one sermon my entire theology turned upside down, and with it my life. The message of Jesus, the whole of Christian faith, is about *living*, not dying. *Today*, not tomorrow. *Here*, not there. It is about faith for the *journey*, not religion for the destination. I am who I am today; I believe what I believe today; I live how I live today, without exaggeration, because of one single sermon.

M. F. Camroux says Harry Emerson Fosdick understood the limitations of preaching, comparing it to a person at a third-story window letting go a drop of medicine in the hope that it would land in the eye of an ailing person in the crowd below.

If I was the only person who ever got a full dose of eye salve from Ken Chafin's third-story window, I would say it was worth every hour he spent in sermon preparation, and if I could only change one life in the course of my life's work, it would be worth it for me as well.

I preach because I know that one sermon can change your life.

I believe in the power of the sermon. I am called to its joys. I am sentenced by its responsibilities. I believe that mere words, spoken from one person to another, can change the shape of our world, our understanding of humanity, our picture of God, and in so doing, *words* can change our lives. But what I believe ultimately about the sermon is that it's not my sermon. It's never *my* sermon, as if some truth delivered from on high. Kathleen Norris says, "The sermon is an oral art form, always more of a thought-in-progress rather than a finished product…. The listener is the one who completes the work."[13]

So the sermon is *our* sermon. What *did* you hear? How will *you* interact *with* it? How will any particular mere words from my mouth inform your thinking, your acting, your faith, your life? And how will you, in turn, inform my life? I preach to a captive audience. For whatever reason you are here, you are here. But *you* preach too. And your words, spoken in the midst of life in "the real world," have much more power to effect real change in our world.

Mark says, strikingly, *Jesus came, preaching.* And so should we. The kingdom is here! Change your life! Believe in yourself and one another and God and goodness and hope and faith and love and forgiveness, and believe in today…and tomorrow will take care of itself!

So join me in the joyful call. And let me impose upon you the life sentence: "Preach the gospel always. And, if necessary, use words."[14]

May it be so!

Notes

[1] Mary Oliver, "The Summer Day," *Poetry 180: A Poem a Day for American High Schools,* Hosted by Billy Collins, https://www.loc.gov/poetry/180/133.html.

[2] In *Strong's Concordance* word #4982 is *sozo,* "from a primary *sos* (contraction for obsolete saos, 'safe'); to save, i.e. deliver or protect (literally or figuratively):—heal, preserve, save (self), do well, be (make) whole."

[3] I did not mention this in the sermon, but I have been told that the language used here is the language of sexual violation, something akin to rape. The prophet laments that God has imposed the divine will over his own—he had no choice in response.

[4] In place of the traditional call/response to the reading of Scripture, we use: "You have heard the ancient story. Let us listen now for the Word of the Lord." We have an ongoing conversation to explain why we believe this response is more theologically accurate than to simply say, "This is the Word of the Lord." See footnote 9 in the preceding chapter.

[5] Much to the chagrin of ministers of music and other associates in ministry, we used to speak of going to church as "going to preaching."

[6] In one of his books, the late John Claypool refers to ministry as the act of staying close to God, staying close to people, and helping people stay close to God.

[7] Thomas Long, *The Witness of Preaching,* 3rd ed. (Louisville, KY: Westminster John Knox Press, 2016), 19.

[8] I have read that Karl Barth, the great theologian of the last century, once remarked after only a few months in the pulpit that he had already said everything he knew to say!

[9] Quoted by Thomas Long. See note 7 above.

[10] The sermon was, admittedly, not an easy one, which I had titled "Damned for the Glory of God: Jesus as Disciple."

[11] The opening meditational thought in today's order of service was this, from Craig Brian Larson, "The Power of Mere Words," *Christianity Today,* (Winter 1997: Change & Opportunity, January 1, 1997), https://www.christianitytoday.com/pastors/1997/winter/7l1033.html:
"Given our turbo-powered world of communications, on occasion I've wondered if [preaching can compete].... Preaching is as low-tech and scant-budget as it gets. Most of my listeners are accustomed to movies powered by special effects, by Hollywood budgets that can soar beyond $100 million.... Can preachers compete? The question stares me in the face: When I take my stand

behind the podium and for some thirty minutes do nothing more than talk, can mere words engage listeners and, more important, change lives?"

[12] "M.F. Camroux, "Preaching to Human Need," *Expository Times*, (December 1998), https://journals.sagepub.com/doi/10.1177/001452469811000304. "The temptation is to try and ignore the depth of the challenge and offer a 'dumbed down' Christianity which shuts out the awkward question and settles for simple palliatives and emotional escapism. If we do that we shall simply dig ourselves into a deeper and deeper hole. If in our preaching we are to make belief in god credible and keep hope alive the real questions must be faced with passionate honesty.... The temptation is to try and ignore the depth of the challenge and offer a 'dumbed down' Christianity which shuts out the awkward question and settles for simple palliatives and emotional escapism. If we do that we shall simply dig ourselves into a deeper and deeper hole. If in our preaching we are to make belief in God credible and keep hope alive the real questions must be faced with passionate honesty."

[13] Kathleen Norris, *Amazing Grace: A Vocabulary of Faith*, (New York: Riverhead Books, 1998), 182. This, also, from Richard Lischer: "The sermon is better viewed as an experiential process of discovery than a proclamation, a process whose end is self-recognition, repentance, new vision, and participation in the life of the community. Narrative preaching does not proceed from above. The word does not knife downward through history toward its target as much as it rises from below out of the shared humanity and Christian identity of its hearers."

[14] Attributed to St. Francis of Assisi.

A New Discipline: A Walk of Joyful Struggle

Questions to Consider

Write a phrase or sentence that characterizes the state and shape of your faith.

How would you characterize the "pace" of your faith (sitting, walking, running, sprinting)?

The story of Jacob wrestling with God on the bank of that river is at the heart of our story of faith. His name was changed that night to Israel, "one who contends with God and prevails." So wrestling with God is at the heart of our faith. How much wrestling have you done?

Is faith supposed to be easy? Would it be better if it were?

The old hymn is titled "Blessed Assurance." How much assurance does faith give you? How does faith help you deal with the uncertainties of life?

Do you have any questions of God that you've never faced honestly? Would you be afraid to deal with those questions?

Have your religious experiences (through church, ministers, teachers) helped you grow? With more knowledge? In spiritual depth?

Can you share your questions freely, even your doubts and concerns, in your faith community?

❖

I want to beg you, as much as I can…, to be patient toward all that is unsolved in your heart and try to love the questions themselves like locked rooms and like books that are written in a very foreign tongue. Do not now seek the answers, which cannot be given you because you would not be able to live them. And the point is, to live everything. Live the questions now. Perhaps you will then gradually, without noticing it, live along some distant day into the answer.
—Rainer Maria Rilke[1]

Amy and I were practically children when we married. I had graduated from Furman in June; she had just finished her sophomore year at Presbyterian College. What were our parents thinking, letting us tie that knot so soon? I repaired computers for two years and installed some of the first networks designed for the personal computer market, introduced in a mostly DOS environment (that was so last century!). Then, after Amy graduated, we loaded my Mazda B2000 pickup and pointed her Dodge Omni toward bluegrass.

Six and a half hours later we were in Louisville, Kentucky, and we pulled into the parking lot of Seminary Village, the post-WWII neighborhood slum that was home to a diverse assortment of impoverished seminarians subsisting on three part-time jobs and monthly support from parents. Luxury apartment "T6" featured one bedroom, a small living space with adjoining dinette, a "one-butt" kitchen, and neighbors so close and so poor that they brought their own plates and silverware for our more-than-weekly meals. We've never been so poor. It was wonderful.

In fall 1988 Southern Baptists were hot in pursuit of institutional inerrancy and the pure (self-)righteousness it would bring. Most of the six SBC seminaries had fallen to the influence of the fundamentalists (we had visited Southeastern Seminary on the day Randall Lolley resigned the school's presidency under pressure), and before we walked for graduation, the Mother Seminary of the convention had also succumbed. We graduated with President Roy Honeycutt's signature on our diplomas and our beloved professors still teaching, but within a few years all had packed their books and retired early or headed for greener pastures.

The strange tensions of a power struggle masquerading as a holy war tinged the lectures in Norton Hall and could be felt in the air just walking across the quad, which the students called "the Josephus Bowl." Silly, destructive Baptist politics notwithstanding, the campus bordered by Lexington Road and Grinstead Drive was holy ground. Our seminary days were golden, glorious.

These institutional tensions on the outside ironically balanced the struggle I had been nurturing within. Maybe there is some undiscovered form of spiritual osmotic pressure that requires an equal balance of theological dis-ease for educational health. Fine-tuned between two poles of concern, without and within, Southern Seminary was the perfect incubator for growth. There was enough pressure on the outside to keep my personal faith from expanding into some grandiose, clerical piety, enough resistance on the inside to prevent a religious implosion due to the weight of institutional dysfunction.

In the first seminary semester "Formations for Christian Ministry" is a required course of study. Helping students prepare emotionally for the intellectual intensity of a three-year curriculum that might challenge core beliefs and deeply held convictions, Formations is somewhat akin to an ongoing session of group therapy. When Amy and I had visited Southern as prospective students, we were still trying to discern the timing of marriage and move and master's degrees. A helpful session in the office of Dr. Wade Rowatt convinced us not to let me go off to seminary while Amy was finishing her last college year, so we married before we moved. Eighteen months later I walked into Formations to find that same friendly face, Dr. Rowatt's same insightful wisdom guiding my formation into ministry.

Early in the semester Dr. Rowatt invited us to consider our own journey of faith—to take a snapshot of the present moment and to describe that "theological selfie" in a phrase. As I reflect on it now, the phrase I chose pretty well captures the introduction and first three chapters of this book (and my theological life at that moment): Into my heart…nothing is ever easy again… looking for the spirit of the message…too many Christians aren't ready to live.

The crisis that had begun one nonchalant day in a Furman convocation was simmering. At times I was intensely aware of a threatening apostasy, but regardless of the temperature at any given moment, I was rarely unaware of it. Like an ever-persistent hangnail, Dr. MacDonald's questions would give me no peace, and the constant debate going on inside my head reminded me the truth of Will Campbell's words: "Once you get educated, nothing is ever easy again." I missed my comfortable answers, my easy faith, so the snapshot of my faith in that moment came rather quickly: "A Walk of Joyful Struggle."

The "walk" reflected my lifelong engagement, beginning with a simple, devotional sincerity in Christian faith ("into my heart"). The intrusion of a cross-examination into the trial of an unexamined faith, of having to find new meaning in old conviction and older scriptures, led to that very palpable sense of "struggle" I was then experiencing ("nothing is ever easy again" and "looking for the spirit of the message"). Even in the frustrating and frightful moments, however, a new understanding was giving a new sense of purpose, a "telos" I had never known. Despite the struggle there was direction and movement to my faith. That new future, a theological "eschatology" that was developing in my understanding, was a guard against the erosion of faith into agnosticism or despair ("too many Christians aren't ready to live"). Despite the struggle, then,

I never lost the joy; it still pulsed beneath, motivating the next steps in that journey that has proven never boring and never ending.

> *"The same night [Jacob] got up and took his two wives, his two maids, and his eleven children, and crossed the ford of the Jabbok. He took them and sent them across the stream, and likewise everything that he had. Jacob was left alone; and a man wrestled with him until daybreak. When the man saw that he did not prevail against Jacob, he struck him on the hip socket; and Jacob's hip was put out of joint as he wrestled with him. Then he said, 'Let me go, for the day is breaking.' But Jacob said, 'I will not let you go, unless you bless me.' So he said to him, 'What is your name?' And he said, 'Jacob.' Then the man said, 'You shall no longer be called Jacob, but Israel, for you have striven with God and with humans, and have prevailed.' Then Jacob asked him, 'Please tell me your name.' But he said, 'Why is it that you ask my name?' And there he blessed him. So Jacob called the place Peniel, saying, 'For I have seen God face to face, and yet my life is preserved.' The sun rose upon him as he passed Peniel, limping because of his hip. Therefore to this day the Israelites do not eat the thigh muscle that is on the hip socket, because he struck Jacob on the hip socket at the thigh muscle."* (Genesis 32:22-32)

I had never understood Jacob until I doubted God. Conversely, I had never understood faith until I realized Jacob isn't just some historical character who spent a night fighting an unknown assailant on a riverbank in the Jordanian countryside. Jacob was me. Jacob is all of us who choose to try to *"walk by faith, not by sight"* (2 Cor 5:7). He is not an exemplar of faith; his story is faith, the life of faithful discipline. Call it history if you must, but it's more than that. It's myth and metaphor, legend and oral tradition (or history layered with all that), and there's never an easy line between the fact and the fiction, the history and the theology. Truth always comes wrapped in narrative; story has always been the best vehicle for communicating the indescribable. His story has a clear, indispensable meaning.

Faith is struggle.

Faith is not easy belief, blind acceptance, comfortable trust. Faith isn't the affirmation of a list of doctrines, mental assent to a set of ideas—that kind of head belief falls within the auspices of religion, and religion is essential to human health and success. We need rites and rituals, outward expressions, language that attempts to give description to the indescribable.

Religion is powerful and important, but the temptation has always been to make religion easy (easy belief, blind acceptance, comfortable trust). There's an enthusiasm that can make believing the unbelievable exciting. Nothing is necessarily wrong with that, but that excitement can be dangerous because the power-hungry are always eager to find tools to manipulate, and excitement is a powerful tool to motivate the masses. The power of religion is that it is intoxicating, possessing, all-encompassing, but hidden in the seed of that power is the potential for its great weakness too.

Religion is an accompaniment of faith, a partner, but the two should never be confused. And while religion can be made easy, faith, according to old Jacob, is always a struggle. Faith is struggle. That's what it means. That's what it is.

Faith *is* wrestling with God.

The story envisions a man, presumably approaching Jacob in the darkness of night, a stranger, confronting him, engaging him in a life-or-death struggle, but that unnamed aggressor cannot gain the upper hand. His surprise attack, his tactics, his strength are no match for the native integrity of our hero, who is the father of the twelve, the ancestor of a nation. What he gives his offspring, all of us, is not physical strength, but integrity for the struggle. In his integrity we inherit the right, if not the will, to wrestle with God and one another and to prevail.

It is worth noting that though Jacob doesn't initiate this encounter, nonetheless, he becomes the aggressor. While the stranger has attacked him, it is he who takes the upper hand and refuses to let go. Jacob will not give up the fight without a blessing. How odd that the victim of an unprovoked attack would demand of his attacker a blessing!

So it is with faith. Though many of us are given the discipline by observant parents (we can inherit the outward expressions that lead to faith), the real encounter comes only through unprovoked struggle. Some moment of crisis calls into question this life we've inherited, the assumptions we've made, the givens we've assumed, and it's "on"! Without the struggle, faith can be practiced as a religious devotion, but faith is only proven, only made true, through the fires of trial. Faith comes unprovoked, but, finally, it remains up to us to recognize the gravity of the moment, to turn the table on our "opponent" (who turns out to be our greatest benefactor), to claim the moment of opportunity and demand, out of the process of struggle, a blessing.

Jacob teaches us that faith is the struggle with God. Jacob gives us the insight to believe that in accepting the struggle, in holding on, in demanding a blessing—the struggle itself becomes our blessing. It's not that walking through those trials is enjoyable. The struggle is real. The "dark night of the soul" can be dislocating, terrifying even, and "joy" doesn't mean blissful and superficial happiness. True joy comes in recognizing our place in the narrative, believing we are part of a larger landscape of meaning and purpose, that despite the wearying good and bad of life's inevitability, God is with us.

Israel—"one who contends with God and prevails." The nation, the name, and the faith are synonymous. The inheritance of the Jewish people is this struggle, the birthright, not of being "the chosen" in some elitist claim of exclusive benevolence, but the chosen privilege of struggling with God. Through Jesus, that inheritance extends to Christian faith; by extension I believe it is the meaning of all faith, regardless of the religious wrapping. To be engaged with God is to struggle with things that matter.

Since the Furman day a Tennessee prophet and activist made me realize I was already in the midst of it, the struggle has defined my faith. In some of my weaker moments, I almost wish it were easier, times I almost envy the cocksure certainty of the evangelical passion I once knew, but what I've come to believe is that cocksure certainty is not faith. Certainty is the province of religion. It's what makes religion intoxicating—and dangerous. Uncertainty, the energy of not knowing, is what makes faith the real and energizing guardian of our souls.

I wouldn't trade this thirty-five-year struggle for any easy certainty. My faith is alive. It is precarious and precious. Real faith ensures persistence and consistency as life throbs with struggle and Spirit, woven together along a step-by-step, day-by-day journey. I'm in it for the long haul. And while it's not all happy, neither is life. Acknowledging that the inevitable, inescapable uncertainties of life are intrinsic to the reality of faith grounds that faith in a God who is incarnate, who is in this very real, very difficult, very celebratory life. God is with us here, now, literally. Faith isn't about there and then; it's not an escapist hope.

God is with us. But that doesn't make life or faith easy.

Welcome to the struggle.

On Controlling the Faithful

Hebrews 6:1–8

Russ Dean, April 24, 2016

Amy and I served two churches in Birmingham when Park Road called us. We had been increasingly frustrated with the lack of depth we experienced in those churches. We wanted more challenge in expressing gospel goodness as a congregation, and we wanted more depth from studies and sermons, a more honest theological dialogue. Our experience formed the background for our growing conviction to pursue this shared pastoral ministry. We enjoyed those churches, but were not content, so we talked a great deal about what we would do if we were pastors, how we would lead, what we would teach, the questions and the honesty we would offer.

We had a ministerial colleague who had been a friend and mentor, so I asked him one day. I remember having been particularly frustrated with most of the sermons I was hearing. Many reflected a safe kind of Baptist "party line." They didn't engage current issues. They didn't struggle with existential questions (suffering and doubt and fear and insecurity). They didn't challenge; they just offered answers. So I asked my friend, "How do you know how much to share from your own experience? Everyone who has been to seminary has some questions to ask. Can you be honest about these questions, the challenges of faith, about theological issues?"

He didn't hesitate, didn't seem to offer his response with remorse; it was just matter-of-fact: "You can never be completely honest about certain things. People just can't handle that."

You never can be honest with church people—*you* can't handle that. Wow.

The response made me sad. Ministers aren't different from anyone else in the world—so if we have questions about theology and the practice of faith and about our world and God, then everyone else has the same questions. (Now, I have no doubt most of us think more about these questions than most of you—shouldn't we? And shouldn't we think more about them *in order* to talk about them?) If the people who are trained to lead the church can never be honest about the real challenges of the life of faith, what does this say about the integrity of the church we have inherited and the church we are creating? Does a church built on such a shallow foundation even have a future? And is it *real* faith we're offering if we can't expose it to *real* questions?

As I look back on my life, this is one of my defining moments. It is why I so often am drawn to challenging texts and issues. (Let me be clear, I am not saying that church should always be hard, that we need to constantly wrestle with thorny issues, always lean into skepticism and doubts—but if we are going to be the church, we cannot avoid conversations just because they are honest.) I determined on that day that if I ever became a pastor, my friend's philosophy would not be my own; that if I were ever a pastor, I would always be completely honest with you on any and every issue. If you don't really want to know what I really think about…hell or resurrection or immigration or HB2[2]…don't ask! And if you're just expecting me, because I'm a minister, to give the party line (if you already know the answer)…don't ask!

My conviction about church begins here: that we must never avoid the struggle of faith because it's easier to live in the warm cozy of preconceived answers.[3] A conviction I hold in *tandem* with that is that I know you are at least as smart as your ministers. I believe lay people can, and should, engage faith at a level that is proportionate to your education and experience and intellect. Adults need to be asking adult questions, not just reciting Sunday school answers. I am convinced a significant portion of those who are leaving church today do so because the church has failed to make itself real, has failed to be a sanctuary for dealing with the hard questions of real lives, and, failing to be a place where people can deal honestly with life, they walk away. (Now, it's not as if they're getting more substance staying in bed or enjoying Starbucks, but that hypocrisy is for another sermon!)

Fred Craddock has been called the preachers' preacher, and he writes of today's interesting text: "Many pastors have yet to appreciate the levels of maturity that laity can attain when the resources for growth are shared patiently and pastorally."[4] I share the Baptist conviction that our most significant resource for growth is the Bible. It's not the *only* authority we should seek, but neither have we come close to exhausting this well of deep wisdom. In this past Wednesday night's excellent discussion of mercy in economics, our own Mark Cramer essentially ended his presentation by asking, "What is the responsibility of the wealthiest county in North Carolina for the poorest?" His question was, "Is Mecklenburg County Robeson County's keeper?"

Of course, this is a biblical question—as all the real questions are. Scripture contains the transcendent stories of all people, every people, facing life's most real, most difficult issues, and seeking a way forward—with God. Cain kills his brother, Abel, out of jealousy, and his pathetic, defensive denial to God

("Am I my brother's keeper?") reveals the shadow side of our humanity. What does it mean to be human? It means to take care of our brother, our sister, whether we are individuals or the most affluent county in the state. Yes, Mark, Mecklenburg County is Robeson County's keeper! We return to the Bible again and again not for some Bible-thumping platitudes, but for time-tested, time-honored wisdom of the deepest kind there is.

Craddock also says many pastors fail to recognize that "withholding [knowledge], no matter how complex…is [just] a means of control."[5] Are we going to be honest…or not? There's a lot of power in standing in this place of authority and defining the narrative for you, and telling you why *you* have to believe it's just as *I* say it is.

I understand that you don't care much about the historical-critical method of biblical interpretation, but if you don't understand that most serious scholars of the Bible have been applying the same critical rules for understanding the Bible as is applied in all other disciplines—and they have been doing this for more than 200 years—if you don't understand that, it will be much more easy for you either to be duped by a charismatic preacher offering easy answers or, if you are a critical thinker, to assume the Bible is outdated gobbledygook that does not pertain to your real life. I'm not willing to live with either of those outcomes.

So this Tuesday, in our coffee and kibitz Bible study, I came across this amazing text in the book of Hebrews: *Therefore, let us go on towards perfection* [which means completeness, not just a pristine idealism] leaving behind *the* basic teaching *about* Christ. Did you hear that? The way toward wholeness is in *leaving behind the basic teaching…about Christ…and repentance…and faith…baptism and* rules about liturgical traditions…*resurrection and eternal judgment* (heaven and hell!).

If I were to stand in most Baptist pulpits today and tell the congregation the only way to become who God intends us to be is to *leave behind the basic teaching* about Christ and heaven and hell—I may not get to the end of the sermon before being shown the door! But I didn't make this up. To leave behind is to go beyond. Some liberals can't go beyond because they give up too soon. Some conservatives can't go beyond because they hang on too long—and both readings are immature.

This writer is pushing us to maturity by urging us to go beyond the basics (which implies that you have to know the basics to begin with), and he points to a nature metaphor as an image of maturity. Ground that receives rain and produces *fruit receives God's blessing*. Just prior to this text he has defined that fruit as the practice of *distinguishing good from evil*. It's that simple—"Do you know right from wrong?"—and yet there is a maturity that so many people cannot find because they are stuck on the basic teachings.

This is so evident in the "culture war" that is raging. When I write and post positions of inclusion and acceptance, most of the social media responses I get are overwhelmingly positive, but there are always the angry voices of Christians who are incensed that I don't know the Bible. Most recently, in the disturbing anger over House Bill 2, I'm being assailed that the Bible says, *God made them male and female*. There's no room for homosexuals and transgender people. Not according to the basic teachings, maybe, but my Bible says we must leave those behind and demonstrate that we have God's law written on our hearts.

That's the key, this writer says, not that we know just enough to quote some scripture, but that we have demonstrated what the prophet Jeremiah claimed more than 500 years before the book of Hebrews was written. There's a covenant that was written on tablets of stone; it's written in the Bible, and that's important—but even 500 years before Jesus, Jeremiah said God has given us a new covenant—and it's not black and white rules; it's a rule of love, and the only place it can be written is on your heart.

It's always been the case, and it's as important now as ever, that the church and its people need to *leave behind the basic teachings about Christ* and move beyond. I know that's a dangerous charge, not one that gives a minister much control over the faithful. But it's the uncontrolled wildfires and uncontrollable love that burn the brightest.

May it be so!

Notes

[1] Rainer Maria Rilke, *Letters to a Young Poet* (United States: Dover Publications, 2019).

[2] "The Public Facilities Privacy and Security Act," or "House Bill 2," was a contentious bill passed by the North Carolina General Assembly in 2016, which, among other things, legislated that in government buildings people could only use restrooms corresponding to the gender indicated on their birth certificates. In March of the following year, the bill was repealed and replaced by House Bill 142.

[3] The opening meditation in today's bulletin was a quotation from Will Campbell, speaking at Furman University, spring term of my freshman year: "Once you get educated, nothing is ever simple again."

[4] Fred B. Craddock, "Hebrews," *The New Interpreter's Bible*, Vol. XII, (Nashville, TN: Abingdon Press, 1998), 72.

[5] Ibid.

A New Dogma:
It's All About Where You Draw Your Lines

Questions to Consider

My wife and I laugh: She's a rule-keeper, and I'm not. We're not talking about breaking the law, but about all the little things—if the recipe calls for one tablespoon, she levels off the top of the measuring spoon with a knife to get an accurate measure; I'm willing to guess a little. How closely do you "toe the line" in the little things?

How much is religion about "the rules" for you?

Do rules limit or liberate? Bind or bless? Constrain or consecrate?

By what "systems" are you defined (gender, religion, citizenship, etc.)? Are the "lines" drawn by these definitions necessary? Are they helpful or restrictive?

Have your "lines" changed in the course of your life (the way you think about relationships, politics, truth, God)?

Is faith a "place to stand" or a "road to walk"? (And what does that have to do with "rules" and "lines"?)

What major "lines" has the church crossed over the centuries? What can this teach us about truth? God? Ourselves?

Is Truth "black and white," "cut and dried," or is there room for some gray area in understanding Truth?

Can you have relationships without rules? What do deep, mature relationships do to "the rules"?

What does the old adage "Rules were meant to be broken!" mean?

❖

Micaela, with four-year-old majesty, has
proclaimed: today, we walk without stepping
On cracks. Sidewalk geometries govern Micaela's
Feet: squares neatly set in lines, by dividers
Foreboding bad luck if you step on the cracks.
When we come to grass, Micaela perplexes,93

Watching me: grass has no geometry,
And what can be met with in grass,
Bites. Less and less, as she grows, Micaela
Will learn to rely on geometries, grids, lines
Dividers, parallels, checks. The consolations
Of geometry serve but to perplex. Life
Is all grass, Micaela, all stepping on cracks.
—*Nancy G. Westerfield*[1]

I used to be a fundamentalist. No, really. This is no criticism of my parents or my church or my religion, but it is the truth. In my childhood everything was cut and dried, left and right, up and down, good and bad, right and wrong. There are rules; we are supposed to follow them.

It was not a bad life (it was actually a pretty good life!). I stayed out of trouble. I went to church. I studied. I did *what* I was supposed to, *when* I was supposed to. There are rules; we are supposed to follow them.

I did not feel constrained by the rules; in fact, they gave a confident energy to life. But there *were* a lot of them. These rules were lines not to be crossed, and most of them were found in the Bible—which meant God was watching. This fact gave a zealous urgency to my personality. As I look back, though I had many good friends, I'm guessing I wasn't everyone's favorite. I was certainly not the life of the party. All eyes did not turn my way when I walked through the door, a rousing cheer rising through the room, like, "Hey, Norm!"[2]

I did not intend to be "holier than thou." At the time I did not think I was, though that might have been a minority opinion! I really did not walk around with a set of self-righteous scales ready to measure everyone. It wasn't that I was judging anyone, as I saw it. It's just that there were rules. And they were pretty clear. There were lines not to cross. And there were a lot of people who crossed them. There were rules.

And the *rules* judged us all.

My education broadened my horizons—which is the difference between education and indoctrination (which just hardens the lines). As my vision expanded, some of those lines began to blur. I began to realize there was some gray there that I had never noticed before. Years ago I was introduced to the music of a Christian contemporary duo who called themselves "Out of the Gray." I loved their music and found their name fascinating, because as I was enjoying their music, I was beginning to realize I was moving in the opposite direction, not out of the gray, but very much into it.

I was beyond that moment of faith crisis,[3] though not completely over it. One of my wife's now-standard pastoral care mantras is, "Time does not heal all wounds, but it does help." Time was helping, and I was beginning to settle into a new normal, into a new comfort level with some of the big questions that had roiled my confidence. I was beginning to see that these questions could engage my faith, not destroy it. Despite the challenge, the doubts, the anxiety, I hadn't thrown it all out.

I have never been close to that. One of the enduring blessings of the faith that was planted so firmly in me by my parents is that my faith has changed, my understanding, my practice—but faith will not let me go. For a very long time I have felt like the old prophet Jeremiah, who said faith was like a fire, shut up in his bones. Even when he became a laughingstock, even when he wanted to let it go, he could not.

I've never been in any danger of letting it go. The closest I've ever come is maybe sometimes wishing I could let it go! There *have* been those moments in which I felt life might be easier if I were not locked in an incessant battle with the questions, if I did not so often struggle with God. And there have been times I felt as if that man on the bank of that river *might* finally let me go… but it has never happened![4]

Despite all that wrestling, though, the truth is that it is all still with me. I'll talk about this more in the final chapter, but I still believe (maybe?) everything I was taught to believe as a child. I just believe all of it differently. Faith still makes sense. Faith still gives meaning. Faith still brings joy. I still want to claim it, follow it, live it, love it.

So in that sense the lines are all still there. That there *are* boundaries seems undeniable to me. To have an identity, any identity, is to be defined by *something*, to draw some lines, or at least to acknowledge the lines someone else has drawn. To be male is not to be female. To be cisgender is not to be transgender. To be Canadian is not to be Mexican. To be communist is not to be capitalist.

To be Christian is to accept certain tenets, affirmations, definitions—even if we need to be in dialogue with our theology, pushing and pulling on the lines. By definition, however, there are lines, distinctions, dividers—there must be—and this need not be a bad thing. We need to understand the lines, however—where they came from, what purpose they serve, how they can strengthen life and faith, and how they can constrain and constrict.

The year before Amy and I went to Southern Seminary, I was participating in an outdoor leadership laboratory. The event was taking place at a Baptist boys' camp in the thick, laurelled wood of the South Carolina mountains. Those ancient Appalachian hills, worn by the slow eons of a steady evolution, are the home to copperheads and katydids, redwood and rhododendron, cold mountain streams and a church camp in every holler.

We were gathered to explore the adventures of the ropes course and cooperative skills, "trust" initiatives, not competitive sports. Sitting at the table in the screened-in dining hall one day, I met a charismatic, wiry triathlete who would later become my boss and best friend. He would become the director of a state-of-the-art health and recreation center that was built on the grounds of the Southern Baptist Theological Seminary during our first year there. I would become his assistant. Technically, I was Terry's secretary, and I enjoyed every one of those secretarial lunches I attended. I was the only male Southern Baptist secretary there. I would not have missed those lunches for the world!

Terry and I were an odd couple. He was raised in Massachusetts ("Mass-a-tu-shits" as we Southerners pronounce it!); I hail from South Carolina. He was raised Roman Catholic (being Baptist was a conversion of mind and heart); I've got Baptist in my blood all the way to back to our founder, John (the Baptist!). He was a footloose and fancy-free bachelor; I was a newlywed. He was an aerobic fitness nut; I was a team sports guy. He was a cradle roll liberal who found Jesus. I was Raised Right[5] and was moving left. When we found each other, it's probably safe to say we were both wandering in the wilderness between these two poles of the journey.

There was an energy to Terry's faith that was enticing. He was grounded in the rhythms of his sacramental christening, but there was a mature freedom to Terry's soul, a spirit and a religious maturity I had never experienced in a close personal friendship.

He tried to teach me to ride a bike; I tried to teach him to play tennis. In thirty years of boat ownership and avid waterskiing, he is one of only two people I have ever had to take to the emergency room! We worked together, played together, ate tuna spaghetti together during one of those health-food kicks Terry was going through. Tuna spaghetti, in case you are curious, is fat-free, chocked full of protein—and tastes just as bad as it sounds! We double-dated, though my date was always the same girl. We studied, debated, explored faith together.

Terry was ahead of me—not just on a bicycle and our scores on the GRE. As we walked together through those challenging and liberating seminary days, he led the way with his openness to question, his willingness to explore, his courage to commit. I don't remember where we were or the specific conversation, but like most of our talks those days, it had something to do with an exploration of the journeys that were taking us both in surprising directions. I am sure that I was being pushed, challenged, by a professor or an idea, being confronted with a new thought that might again cause me to rethink yet another of my firm beliefs. At the apex of one of those discussions, Terry O'Toole looked at me, and with his characteristic Irish grin he said, "Dino, it's all a matter of where you draw the lines."

It's where you draw your lines.

Since my Furman days I had heard conservatives warning about, and railing against, "relativism," and when Terry made that comment, I have to admit that I did inhale just a little bit: Was my friend a relativist? And would I soon be headed to hell down that slippery slope too?

I hope I'm not headed to hell, though I *have* decided that "slippery slope" is actually a pretty good metaphor for faith! If you don't keep moving, yes, you will lose ground. It *is* slippery—but isn't a call to active movement better than standing still on the supposed "solid ground" of convenience or certitude or apathy? Is this really how we want to describe faith? And I am definitely a relativist—as are even the most rabid Christian fundamentalists.[6] If we will all be honest, we will have to recognize and acknowledge that the lines keep changing—for all of us. As we keep walking into the inevitable future, God keeps opening our eyes. Most Christians, even fundamentalists, for example, no longer champion slavery, though that was once an inviolable tenet of Southern doctrine. (So what about *that* line?.. It moved!)

Even though they claim an unwavering confidence of belief in the absolute fundamentals of faith, fundamentalists cannot decide among themselves exactly how many (and which) tenets of faith are to be regarded as fundamental! Evangelicals do not agree on the charismatic gifts, and they spar over Calvinism. Do we immerse or sprinkle or effuse (pour water over the head—and is it once or thrice)? Or can you get to heaven drip dry? Where do you draw that line? There are even vigorous conversations in some evangelical circles about such topics as environmentalism and atonement theory ("nothing but the blood"… really?).

We are all relativists. It's just a matter of where you draw your lines.

What Terry made me see in that off-the-cuff remark is that the lines—all the lines—are arbitrary. Though we claim our beliefs with conviction, often citing an objective authority such as a theological expert or a primary source, church history and tradition, or Scripture (often citing chapter and verse), even the best-trained, the most well-studied, the most firmly devout among us cannot agree on, well, much of anything! It's all a matter of where we draw the lines—which are unavoidably and unalterably personal and subjective, based on our experience and the prejudices that flow from that experience, and influenced by our education and our always limited sight.

In that moment I learned a little bit about Truth, and I learned a lot about humility!

Truth doesn't change, but since our view is so narrow, depending on where we are on the twisty, winding journey up that mountain called faith, sometimes our glimpse of truth appears out of one window and sometimes out of another. Occasionally we may even catch a glimpse out of the rearview mirror.

Terry was right, and in that moment it was as if he drew a line in the sand of faith (wait, it's not a solid rock?[7]), and he dared me to step over it. Surprisingly, what I found when I stepped over it, as I have several times since then, was not apostasy, the denial of God, the erosion of faith; what I found was a new land of exploration—a new, exciting world in which my faith has continually expanded and deepened.

A fundamentalist theology claims that the lines deepen our faith and our life—when we stay within them. In this understanding, only by knowing the limitations imposed by God can we know God's divine bounty. My experience tells me the opposite. We do not cross the lines with a defiant, rebellious spirit, but they do beckon us to push the limits and explore.

The lines have not gone away for me. It is not as if I believe there should be no rules, that all convictions are equally valid, that "anything goes." The lines have *not* gone away for me, but, thanks to Terry, they did change. Rather than precisely defined borderlines, impenetrable walls, unalterable precepts, the lines have become a kind of *borderland*, wide and fertile. The lines now open onto fields with expansive views and deep forests, tangles of dog hobble and undergrowth. There are cliffs and streams and rocks. The lines, which have become wild lands of exploration, have become my favorite terrain. They are neutral no man's lands. They are the gateway to a world of invitation and discovery.

There are more borderlands than there are borderlines. It is not as if someone is just musical or just athletic, just intellectual or just mechanical, just
artistic or just mathematical. Our gifts and identities blend and merge and
cross over. There are borderlands between them, and the more we learn about
our biology, the more evident this is going to be. Our sexuality, for example,
is not just a bifurcation of male and female. The animal kingdom displays an
incredible diversity of sexuality—heterosexuality and homosexuality, asexual-
ity and bisexuality and transsexuality.

We are "red and yellow, black and white," but not just red, yellow, black,
or white. What about the lines between those colors? Where did they come
from? What do they mean? Gone are the days, thanks be to God, of defining
an American "negro" as someone with 1/8 or more black blood. Maybe all that
can save our destructive racial bias, the original sin of a nation built largely on
the backs of slave labor, is a mulatto justice, a blending of the colors into one.

One love. One blood. One life. You got to do what you should.

One life with each other, sisters, brothers.

One life, but we're not the same.

We get to carry each other, carry each other.

One. One.[8]

There is humanity and there is divinity—but the incarnational theology
of our Jesus story is a hint that perhaps even those categories are not so far
apart that "ne'er the twain shall meet." Christian orthodoxy says Jesus was fully
human and fully divine. When we say "I'm only *human*," we are usually referring to our weaknesses, our separation from God. When we say *he* was *fully*
human, we mean exactly the opposite.

Theologian and author Walter Wink says there is another way to think
about humanity and divinity. He takes this clue from the strange vision of
Ezekiel, who looked into the heart of that theophany and saw that the creatures at the center of it "*were of human form*" (Ezek 1:5). Wink notes how odd
it is that at the center of a vision of God is not a "divine being" but a human
one. He takes deep insight from that vision and challenges us to reconsider our
understandings of humanity and divinity:

> If God is in some sense true humanness, then divinity inverts itself.
> Divinity is not a qualitatively different reality; quite the reverse, divin-
> ity is fully realized humanity. Only God is, as it were, Human. The
> goal of life then, is not to become something we are not—divine—

but to become what we truly are—human. We are not required to become divine: flawless, perfect, without blemish. We are invited simply to become human, which means growing through our sins and mistakes, learning by trial and error, being redeemed over and over from compulsive behavior—becoming ourselves, scars and all. It means embracing and transforming those elements in us that we find unacceptable. It means giving up pretending to be good and, instead, becoming real.... In this vision, then, the "one in human form" represents the archetypal image, "as it were," of fully human being, reaching out to Ezekiel with a seemingly impossible task: that of becoming human.[9]

This confusion of humanity and divinity has always been part of the conversation in Christian theology. There are other similar quotations, but to give one example, Clement of Alexandria (c. 150–215), one of the early "church fathers," wrote, "Yea, I say, the Word of God became a man so that you might learn from a man how to become a god." Talk about a confusion of lines!

Maybe Jesus's purpose was to teach us how to live into that divine birthright, the *imago dei*, the image of God in which we were created. I am not God. And God is not human. But many of the world's great mystics have explored that borderland between the two. Maybe it's not heresy to think of that space as a land of exploration, not some impenetrable barrier.

A few years ago we officiated the wedding of my sister's older child, the oldest of my parents' grandchildren, who was the first to cross that borderland into the fecund landscape called marriage. It was a destination wedding, and what a destination! Along the shore on the border between Georgia and South Carolina, there is a little patch of heaven called Debordieu. We referred to that name during the wedding homily as these two separate and distinct individuals, male and female, Southerner and Yankee, Democrat and Republican, liberal and conservative, stood at the altar on the sacred border where the "*two shall become one flesh*"(Mark 10:8). We noted that this sacred crossing of lines, this merging of disparate identities, was coming at a place named in 1777 by the French explorer Marquis de Lafayette "the borderland of God."

Maybe each line is—every single one—a borderland of God. Maybe each line is an expanse of terrain that beckons to be explored, charted, but never tamed. The old joke asks: How far can a dog walk into the woods? The answer is halfway—because once it crosses the midway point, it is walking *out* of the woods! But there is no such divide in the borderlands of our explorations into faith. There is no middle ground, no way out! It's more like trying to divide the number into two pieces. When you do this, each piece has the same number of points with which you started. Each tiny piece of the number line contains an infinite expanse.

There are lines, but they need not frustrate us individually or divide us corporately. Though these borders between concepts and convictions are often characterized as absolute, defining, dividing lines, they are really lands, the fertile, sacred ground of our spiritual growth.

"It's all a matter where you draw the lines." Yes, Terry. Thank you!

So draw your lines. We all have them. Draw them with conviction. And draw them in humility—because you never know when God is going to call you to cross over one and into a whole new land of exploration!

Welcome to the journey.

Rules and Right—It's All Grass

Micah 6:1–8; Matthew 5:1–12

Russ Dean, February 3, 2002

I love Nancy Westerfield's poem about little four-year-old Micaela—and how I can relate to her dilemma! Since childhood, I too have been a watcher of sidewalk cracks. Whether stepping on every one or avoiding them all, my eyes are still drawn down, my steps still paced by these annoying "geometries" as Westerfield calls them. In the movie *As Good as It Gets*, Jack Nicholson plays an obsessive-compulsive writer named Melvin Udall. Udall also suffers this crack-stepping phobia, and in one wonderful scene he hobbles down the street with his new girlfriend, played by Helen Hunt, painstakingly, psychotically avoiding every crevice, only to enter her home to find her floors a mosaic of tiny little octagonal tiles…lines everywhere!

The story of the people of God could be told, I think, as the diagnosis of "sidewalk-crack-aphobia," because the pull of those "sidewalk geometries" has always been with us.

When God called Abram, the covenant was simple: "*I am God Almighty; walk before me, and be blameless. And I will make my covenant between me and you, and will make you exceedingly numerous* "(Gen 17:1–2). Isn't that amazing?

No "thou shalt nots." No geometries. No cracks. No rules—just right. God invites relationship—*walk before me.*

As you know from reading the scriptures and from your own pilgrimage, that walk is a difficult journey at times. And when the Israelites stumbled, in one way or another they demanded of God some definitions: "What is a 'covenant' anyway? What do you mean, *Walk before me?* How 'blameless' is 'blameless'? Give us some boundaries. We need some rules. Where exactly are those cracks?"

If you listen closely, I think you can still hear reluctance in God's voice in these words spoken to Moses just before the giving of the Ten Commandments: "*Say to the house of Jacob...I bore you on eagles' wings, and brought you to myself. Now therefore, if you obey my voice and keep my* covenant (not my commandments...not my rules...God says, "Just walk with me!"), *you shall be my treasured possession out of all the peoples.... You shall be a priestly kingdom and a holy nation*" (Exod 19:4–6). But the people still stumbled and grumbled, so God finally consented. Here are the rules: *You shall have no other gods.... You shall not make any graven images.... You shall not take the name of the LORD in vain.... You shall not kill* (Exod 20).

There you have it. The beginning of our religious "sidewalk geometry." Cracks to be avoided. Cracks to be evaded. Cracks to lure our eyes. Cracks to limit our steps. Cracks to alter our natural gait. "Step on a crack...break your momma's back!"

The Jews called these "cracks" *the Law*, and the Law became the centerpiece of the religion. The entire cultic practice of Judaism, eventually culminating in the elaborate worship in an elaborate temple, was built around keeping the Law. And from that rather simple declaration of Ten Commandments, the Jews developed 613 laws—interpretations of interpretations, definitions of definitions, cracks upon cracks upon cracks.

Such legalism has been a persistent cry of religious people, but faithfulness to God cannot be defined simply by a list of "dos and don'ts." For in so trying to legislate our morality before God, we inevitably turn the Law itself into a god. The Law becomes a stricture, a constraint, a limit, which keeps us bound, and though there is good which can come from such binding, we must always listen for the original call, for the voice of God, which still calls to us: "*I am God Almighty;* [just] *walk before me, and be blameless. And I will make my covenant between me and you, and will make you exceedingly numerous*" (Gen 17:1–2).

The prophet Micah was fed up with the pious moralizing and moralism of his people. He preached in the eighth century B.C.E., a time of economic and political affluence for the people of Israel. The theology of the religious elite justified their wealth, their power, and their comfort, and the rules suited them just fine, because they heard in them what they wanted to hear. Speaking in the voice of God, Micah offers sarcasm for their obedience: *With what shall I come before the LORD? Shall I bring burnt offerings?... Calves?... Rams?... Oil?... Will God require the sacrifice of my own child?*

Of course, the Law *did* require the offerings which Micah mocks (except for the sacrifice of children, which simply serves to highlight his cynicism), but he makes it clear—God is not pleased with sacrifice, with hoops jumped and cracks avoided—if our hearts are not right. Just do what is *right*, Micah says: *Justice...mercy...walk with God.*

Gary Badcock says, "Religious life is about participation in the primordial mystery of God through prayer, worship, and lifestyle, all of which involves so much more than bare knowledge (or, to paraphrase, 'obedience'). Religion relates to fundamental issues of life and death, to what it is to be a human being, and to what it is *to live in relationship to God.*"[10]

One of the recent advertising slogans for Outback Steakhouse declares boldly, "No Rules. Just Right." So it is, I believe, with our life with God. We will not please God living by the rules. But when we walk together, life— divine and human—will be just right.

Shortly after enrolling at the Southern Baptist Theological Seminary in Louisville, Kentucky, the campus underwent major cosmetic surgery. The small gymnasium was partially raised, and an $11 million health and recreation facility was annexed to the old gym. For over a year the campus was in a construction uproar, but after the new facility was completed, the sidewalks had been poured, and new grass was sown, we began to notice signs on the lawn: "Please Walk on Grass—But Don't Make Paths!"

The minister to the seminary preached a sermon that fall, with that same title, in which he challenged his community to a life of freedom, to a life of creativity, to a life of nonconformity, to a life of walking in the grass. Creatures of habits, we fall in line too quickly, without even thinking, and like one of the hapless herd, we walk the same route day after day until the grass has been replaced by the hard-packed ground—we might as well be on the sidewalk again, watching for the cracks.

But God called us to be free, to walk in the grass, to learn, to love, to live.

Augustine said, "Love God—and do *as you will*." I'm guessing that I'm not the only Baptist who learned to walk on the sidewalk, carefully, dancing between the cracks, and wondering what in the world was going on out there on the lawn. What an amazing lesson it was for me to come to believe that God loves us not *because* of what we do (or don't do), but that God loves us—like we parents love—*just because*. And if I could learn to love God, to really love God with *heart, soul, mind, and strength*, I really could walk where I wanted to, and God would always be right there with me.

Jesus says that God's blessing comes not to those who live by the letter of the Law, as if they are earning some reward, but to the *poor in spirit…the mourners and the meek…the peacemakers and the pure in heart…the persecuted and the merciful…those who hunger and thirst for* right. Walking in the grass frees us from the crippling obligations of the rules, but here's the twist: In the grass, the love of God's freedom and the freedom of God's love are more binding than any simple or blind or fearful obedience could ever imagine. We are bound. But we are bound.

Are you walking down life's sidewalk stumbling over the cracks? Or have you ventured barefoot into the freedom of God's green, green grass?

Just remember: In the grass…it's all cracks!

May it be so. Amen!

Notes

[1] Westerfield, Nancy G. "Not Stepping on Cracks." *Theology Today* 56, no. 2 (July 1999): 247–247. https://doi.org/10.1177/004057369905600212. Reprinted by Permission of SAGE Publications, Ltd.

[2] From the television sitcom *Cheers*.

[3] This is the subject of chapter one, "Once You Get Educated, Nothing Is Ever Easy Again."

[4] In the previous chapter I talk about the story in Genesis 32. That wrestling match on the bank of the Jabbok River, where Jacob's name is changed to Israel ("one who contends with God and prevails"), is a metaphor for the life of faith.

[5] We learned this phrase in one of the books by Ferrol Sams and have used it consistently ever since. We always spell the phrase using capital Rs to indicate something big is at stake when we bring up our children in the life of faith. Obviously, here I am playing on the multilayered meanings of *right*.

[6] In this arena of what might be characterized as Christian apologetics, "relativism" is seen in opposition to the "absolute" claims of doctrine. For the fundamentalist there are lines—God's lines—and there is no room for any relativism. God's truth is static, unchanging, absolute, and this truth is expressed in immutable, literal rules that are crossed only to our eternal peril.

[7] In Matthew 7 Jesus tells a parable of the wise and foolish builders. One built firmly on the rock; the other builder's home was washed away because he built on shifting sand.

[8] U2. "One," *Achtung Baby.* Island, 1991. CD.

[9] Walter Wink, *The Human Being: Jesus and the Enigma of the Son of the Man,* (Minneapolis: Augsburg Books, 2001), 29.

[10] Gary D. Badcock, *The Way of Life: A Theology of Christian Vocation,* (Grand Rapids, MI: Wm. B. Eerdmans Publishing Co., 1998), 132.

A New Theology:
God Always Does Everything God Can Do

Questions to Consider

Has your faith ever been challenged? Have you had a crisis of faith?

What is God? (This is a big question, but have you ever really thought about it? Is God "the man upstairs"? Is God a being with supernatural power? Is God a spirit? Is God Spirit? If "God is love," does this mean love is God? All love?)

Is God all-powerful? What are the full implications of an all-powerful being, outside of space and time, intervening in this world's natural processes?

Does God make specific good things to happen (the winning touchdown, the job promotion)?

Does God *allow* bad things to happen? Does God *cause* bad things to happen? Is there a difference?

If God could stop bad things from happening, why doesn't God do so? (If you could stop a crime and you didn't, could you be prosecuted for criminal negligence?)

What is the difference between love and power? Which is more powerful?

"Power corrupts, and absolute power tends to corrupt absolutely." Could this be true even of God?

Would you rather your parents be all-powerful or have true, unconditional love for you?

❖

The worst of unqualified omnipotence is that it is accompanied
by responsibility for every detail of every happening.
—Alfred North Whitehead, Adventures of Ideas[1]

This book is a testimony to the fact that one message can change your life. One sentence can lodge itself in one of those synaptic gaps in your brain; a simple phrase can wedge its disturbing power in a crevice in your soul—and never leave you alone. Never leave you alone! I am who I am today as a Christian, my convictions are what they are in faith and morality and ethics because at least nine of those scars have been carved into my soul. Nine distinct wounds mark some moment in my journey of faith that broke me open, if only subtly, slowly, quietly.

And then the mysterious power of healing made me stronger.

I have often quoted the lyrics of the singer named Sting in sermons and lessons and, even knowing his convictions are agnostic, sometimes refer to him as my favorite theologian. His music, filled with biblical allusions, knows deep spiritual truth. In "The Lazarus Heart" he sings of the mysterious, paradoxical strength of this healing power of brokenness:

> There was as wound in his flesh so deep and wide.
> From the wound a lovely flower grew
> from somewhere deep inside.[2]

Challenges to my once-comfortable ideas of religion wounded me. One by one the moments I am recalling in this book broke open my faith. If the moments had all come at the same time, if they had not been accompanied by the wise counsel of faithful friends and mentors, those disturbing moments might have done more than put cracks of doubt in my faith. These challenges had the potential to break down my faith. Instead, thanks be to God, "from the wound a lovely flower grew."

One day at the Southern Baptist Theological Seminary my understanding of the very nature of God was challenged. In a lightning-bolt moment the nature of divinity was stripped of the all-encompassing power I had once defended so adamantly. While the challenge was real, a crisis in the making, in that wound my conviction was renewed in time, God was actually reborn, and faith sprouted a new and beautiful meaning in the place where I had known confusion and fear and doubt. And that God, even denuded of the brute force I had once equated with the very name, has become even more "powerful." I begin my book *The Power of the God Who Can't* with these words, as I reflect on the encounter that changed my God forever:

> God is not omnipotent.
> There, I've said it.
> If that first sentence hasn't scared you away or offended your spiritual senses, what you will find in this book is my attempt to tell you what that unorthodox declaration means to me and how I have come to be able to say it, even comfortably enough to make it part of the repertoire of my

public preaching and teaching. I will try to tell you why the statement, "God always does everything God can do," has deepened my faith. And I will try to offer something akin to an old-fashioned "testimony," an apologetic for the God in whom I now place my trust, who is, I believe, more credible to a sophisticated 21st century world, more capable of touching people's real lives in real ways, and…more powerful.

Yes—the God who can't—is more powerful.

This book is a pastor's reflection, not an academic thesis. These chapters chart the journey that began one day in a classroom in Norton Hall on the campus of the Southern Baptist Theological Seminary. Dr. Frank Tupper, lecturing in Systematic Theology, spoke the words too nonchalantly for a room filled with conservative "preacher boys." When he said "God always does everything God can do," and said it so easily ("… everything God can do?"), a little of the air went out of the room. Someone questioned his theology (and maybe his judgment and the integrity of his faith), and an engaged dialogue ensued. It is a dialogue that has never left me.

For many years I wrestled with his words, and with Dr. Tupper's impotent God. I wrestled with this "God who can't" until I became a pastor. In that setting, though, given the privilege and responsibility of preaching, speaking honestly to real people who were living real lives and dealing with real struggles and disappointments, challenges and journeys, so many of the platitudes of faith, which just seem to be part of the Southern air we breathe, felt hollow. I simply could not stand in my pulpit and offer trite clichés, feed my people on a diet of the God who can, but mostly does not. My commitment to speak a realistic word, based on the God I understand through the life of Jesus, to real people living real lives led me back to Dr. Tupper's classroom, and through that pulpit discipline I came to claim his conviction as my own: there are some things God cannot do.

Any friend who could, would.

Any parent who could, would.

Surely a God who could, would, too. Always.

"God always does everything God can do"? That's crazy. God can do *anything*. God can do *everything*. After all, God is…*God*. Right?

I believe we ought to think carefully about that.

Too often, the language of faith is divorced from the real world, the joys and struggles of life as they are actually experienced, by "believers" and "non-believers" alike.[3] We need a "theology of reality"—one bold enough to affirm belief but with a maturity and courage that speaks the truth about what we observe in the world and how it meshes with, or resides in tension with, faith. There are many who will challenge my claim that the language of faith is divorced from reality, and they might challenge this primarily in light of the common usage of religious language.

Inside the "fishbowl" of a near-ubiquitous evangelicalism, people are all too familiar with the too-easy affirmations of religious enthusiasm. I was raised in the fishbowl. Most of the people I have ever known live in it whether they are religious or not. A set of theological conventions representing lowest-common-denominator assumptions abound throughout our religious nation. The ideas are especially strong in our Southern culture, though they are not unique to it.

Like the politician fueling the fire, feeding the frenzy at the stump speech, most preachers know how to get an "Amen." And if they don't get that expected affirmation, sometimes they just ask for it: "Can I get an 'Amen'?" The prompt is hardly needed where I live, however. Stand in most pulpits, or just "preach" from the office water cooler, the bleachers, the cocktail party, and you're guaranteed to get a few "Amen"s if you just say, "Everything happens for a reason." Or just say, "Well, I don't understand (why such and such happened), but I know God is still in control." You'll have a sympathetic audience almost anywhere.

But does that affirmation really match our reality? God is in control? Holocausts and hurricanes and all manner of horrific happenings and... God...is in...control? Really? That mass shooting in an elementary school happened "for a reason"? Really? Is that really what you believe? And if you've never thought about it, stop for just a minute and ask if this makes sense. If it does not actually appear that some divine beneficence is in charge of our world (because our world is filled with violence and division and hatred), should we maintain that belief against all credible evidence to the contrary? Does it benefit our faith to demand that we who believe are perpetually at such odds with reality? Might this make us seem either out of touch or arrogant? Doesn't this view implicitly condemn and criticize all who do not share such a vision of the world?

In his book of daily devotions titled *Listening to Your Life,* in the entry simply titled "Words," Frederick Buechner says,

> Words—especially religious words, words that have to do with the depth of things—get tired and stale the way people do. Find new words…. Arrange the alphabet into words that are true in the sense that they are true to what you experience to be true. If you have to choose between words that mean more than what you have experienced and words that mean less, choose the ones that mean less because that way you leave from for your hearers to move around in and for yourself to more around in too.[4]

The word *omnipotent* is a word that says more than we have experienced. It may sound like powerful piety to some, but to an increasingly sensitive and scientific and skeptical world, to people within and without the church, it rings only of a religiosity devoid of reality. We need to rearrange our alphabet, to find some new words that are true to what we actually experience.

I know some do believe that God is in control of everything at every moment. I know they believe this fervently, but I believe many others have accepted or adopted this common language just because it's in the air. I am convinced many people are uncomfortable with this idea, or would be if they thought they could ever be honest enough to admit it. They believe in God— but they have never been given a reasonable alternative to the common words and ideas about God. In the absence of any other rhetoric, any other theological alternatives, the language and the "God" of all power and control, well, this language controls![5]

I am not suggesting that faith does not give us "eyes" to see differently. It does. It should. I am suggesting that being a person of faith need not make us hopelessly out of touch, completely at odds with obvious reality.

Of course, within Christianity there is a "language of Zion," a language based on the biblical images and unique theological concepts particular to our faith. Every religious tradition has its own unique lexicon. I also understand that within any organization, system, or program, intrinsic to any philosophy or worldview there will always be specific "insider language." And the language of all religious is based on theological affirmations that assume the hope of faith—*"the conviction of things not seen"* (Heb 11:1)—not the empiricism of dispassionate science. I accept that any beliefs that are reliant on a confidence in the *unseen*, a trust in the ineffable God, might be criticized as contradicting reality.

So there is the language of faith in general and the jargon specific to Christianity in particular, but the common vernacular I am questioning, the theological assumptions of the ubiquitous street-level proclamation, is not dependent upon anything as specific as a systematic theology. "God language" will always assume a worldview of faith, a perspective that will not be limited to empirical observation, yet there is no reason the language needs to assume an antagonism to scientific reason and no reason it cannot be honest to our actual experience, even if that experience involves doubt and uncertainty.

One needn't be religious, much less committed to any particular local church; one needn't espouse enough sectarian or denominational dogma to have been indoctrinated in the Church of the Omnipotent Force. As much as it is a theology of Christendom, with its official magisterium, its impressive orthodoxy, the all-powerful God is also a myth of the reigning culture, the absent-but-prevailing God a fixed icon in the corporate consciousness of a religion-drenched people. This all-powerful "God" is certainly the norm, but human history is replete with examples that the normative view is hardly a guarantee of truth or integrity or authenticity!

So in a culture that is so intoxicated with religion, is there a better way to talk about God? Is any other language even possible? Could we give religious and spiritual-but-not-religious[6] people a language that affirms faith, acknowledges the presence of the divine, allows the possibility of transcendence—yet without dismissing their experiences of doubt and deep disappointment? What language of God might invite dialogue even with skeptics? What language might give the church a fulsome defense of faith yet countenance a healthy awareness of the secular wisdoms of the contemporary conversation?

In looking for such a language, the church finds itself at an interesting crossroad, located uncomfortably in the crosshairs of two fundamentalisms, one nascent, the other dying. The first fundamentalists are as religious as the second, though these evangelical atheists would scoff at such a pronouncement with haughty disdain. Of course, there is nothing new about atheism itself, but the movement of the "new atheists" has been born as a response to the older, dying fundamentalism of angry and fearful religious conservatism. The church's inability to discover a language that is as intellectually convincing as it is emotionally inspiring only adds fuel to the condescending fire offered by both sides of the extreme.

The first fundamentalism mocks any and all religious language, and does so with a religious passion. It claims its "objective truth" under the guise of a host of academic-sounding names: "empiricism," "naturalism," "materialism," "reductionism." It makes its claim that this absolute truth is the basis for the only truth that can be trusted (sounds pretty religious, doesn't it?). It offers "meaning" to the human being through the purely random happenstance of human consciousness, despite our pointless end being utter nihilism (and what exactly is *empirical* about "meaning"?). The countering fundamentalism, this one from the righteous right, disdains the objectivism of science, refusing to see that *refusing to see* has always and will always spell the death of any movement, religious or otherwise.

The intersecting commonality of these conflicting fundamentalisms, which makes both of them dangerous because they're so dogmatically religious, is their equally blinding obsession with biblical literalism. One says everything about the Bible is literally wrong—and what's important is to say it is literally wrong. The other says everything about the Bible is literally true—and what's important is to say it is literally true.

Both literalisms are misguided, yet the church has largely failed to teach another way to read its Holy Scripture. There is a better way to read, but in the vacuum left by that failure to educate, a culturally legitimized theology has become dominant in church and culture.

Living in the crucible of conflict, and with a void of critical thinking about biblical language, offering an alternate religious word on anything is a bit tricky. From the one extreme there is no God at all, so no "omnipotence" to reject, no "control" to counter. From the other extreme there is God in everything—the remission from cancer, the winning Super Bowl touchdown, the parking space close to the supermarket door on the day of the pouring rain—all celebrating omnipotence as an unquestioned given in the conversation.

One says: Grow up, children—we'll never get anything we'd like a god to do.

The other says: Accept it on childlike faith—God always does anything God wants to do.

The common misunderstanding of the language expressed by both fundamentalisms, however, also offers a hopeful point of contact, a potential reconciliation in the bitter divorce between the fundamentalisms. That point of contact is God—who is above the "God" largely misunderstood due to an inadequate literacy, a poor hermeneutic. In other words, both fundamentalisms poorly read the Bible! This unfortunate but shared error offers a moment of legitimacy for those of us caught awkwardly between these two vocal and angry worldviews. The hope is to be found in a language of faith that, on the one hand, affirms the reality of science, accepting that which is proven, while allowing *for* God in the beauty and mystery of the unknown (or unknowable?). On the other hand, it is a language that affirms the reality *of* God, accepting that the beauty and mystery of the unknown (or unknowable?) is God, while allowing for uncertainty in that which is proven.

To state it more simply:

There is a language of faith that...

Allows the skeptic to:	*Allows the believer to:*
affirm the reality of science,	affirm the reality of God,
accept that which is proven,	accept that the beauty and mystery
while allowing for God in the	of the unknown
beauty and mystery of the	(or unknowable?) is God
unknown (or unknowable?)	while allowing for uncertainty in
	that which is proven

Or to say it even more simply yet: God always does everything God can do!

God is not the cause of all things, good and bad. The secularist (skeptic, scientist), understanding the laws of nature, knows this to be the case. Believers need the maturity and security to accept that a level of uncertainty is just inherent to this world, but within a framework that does not reject God. Theologies have been created to explain and justify "why bad things happen to good people,"[7] such as has been called "the fall of man." This critical moment is ironically named since if old Eve hadn't taken a bite of that apple, all would have been well![8]

Such a theology ultimately fails even within a framework of faith, however, if we follow such a view to its logical conclusion. If God "created out of nothing" (theologians often retain the Latin *creatio ex nihilo*), setting the world and all its potentials and powers into motion, and defining all the rules pertaining to those potentials and powers, then anything that happens within that system must logically have its origin in God. In such a worldview God would have to be responsible for all the bad things and the evil in the world.

God is not the cause of all things, good and bad—but neither has the possibility of the divine been convincingly eclipsed by science. The believer, understanding the power of faith, knows this to be the case. Skeptics need the maturity and security to accept that beauty and mystery are inherent to this world—and within a framework of humility and creativity and open-ended possibility ought to be willing to consider God. The arguments against God, at least those advanced by the new atheists, are shallow at best. They inveigh against a "God" that many intellectually curious and critical theologians have also long-since rejected. Most of the arguments are based in a rejection of the evils of organized religion. No person of committed faith I know would disagree that religion deserves much of its bad reputation, but it is either intellectually disingenuous or just lazy to cast such an unfair blanket of condemnation across millions of people and centuries of compassion and goodwill, if only those enacted through simple gifts of kindness, motivated by faith.

The "intellectual" arguments against God are as old and weary as bad theology—and the skeptic, often educated and sometimes just a little bit too superior in attitude, owes it to the integrity of her smarts to do a bit more homework. If I wanted to take up an argument against science based on scientists with only a fifth-grade education, or an argument based against those who have used their vast knowledge only to create the atomic bomb, biological weapons, or computer viruses, I could make a pretty good case that all science is shallow and wicked. It would be neither true nor fair, but I could make that case. So it is with most "intellectual" arguments against God.

None of the possible conclusions to this confusion is acceptable to me. I will not simply lean on a "blind faith," rejecting obvious evidence (as science sees the world), to defend a God we just cannot understand. Neither can I reject the notion of God out of hand. I accept neither the skepticism nor the theology whose logical conclusions lead to an unacceptable and unnecessary definition of God. I will not accept these options, because there is another option: God always does everything God can do.

This idea may sound like heresy. I believe it is not. It may be a radical departure from your customary way of thinking of God, but "from the wound a lovely flower grew." Discovering (rediscovering?) the God who is only love, who always does everything love can do, is the blossom of insight and inspiration that might offer a lifesaving way forward for the church. It is insight and inspiration we need as we continue into a future that will never turn its back on the hard-earned inheritance bequeathed by the scientific method. And the God who is always and only love, never just Omnipotent Force, offers an important way forward as humanity, skeptic and believer alike, step into a future that will never completely turn its back on God.

Religion is born of the sense of awe, the hint of transcendence that comes to human beings in unsuspecting moments—and science will never know so much as to eliminate that innate and fundamental response. Wouldn't even that one simple, beautiful equation that some scientists believe is discoverable, one equation explaining everything, wouldn't even such an "explanation" provoke deep and inspiring awe? And wouldn't such a final "answer" evoke even more questions (How? Why? Who?)?

The way forward is not to be found in rejecting God. The religious impulse is just too deeply imbedded in the human soul. But neither is the future of humanity to be found in rejecting science and expecting people to accept and affirm a "reality" that is increasingly at odds with reason and experience. There is a better way.

As I noted in my book *The Power of the God Who Can't,*

> To accept this theology, we will have to give up that so-called "personal God," the "man upstairs" who can be manipulated by our fears and prayers to shape the events of this world in our favor, to bend natural laws (regardless what effect that may have on other people) for our isolated benefit. Yes, we will lose that "God" in a new theology, but in its place we will gain an appreciation for Spirit and Mystery and Movement and Love. Presence *is* work. If you do not believe that, you have never sat quietly with a loved one, silently, doing "nothing" but attending to the grief of heartache or loss. If you have been on the receiving end of such a labor of love, you know there is nothing greater than the active power of silent presence.
>
> Consider the following thought experiment as a kind of "proof" of this logic. Suppose I was diagnosed with a terminal cancer tomorrow. God forbid, but what would happen? What would I hope for? What might I expect, especially, using this thought experiment, from my parents? They brought me into this world. I am, quite literally, created by them, in their image. They raised me, loved me, provided for me, cared for me. Then they set me free. Through the complexity of genetic heritage, they may in fact be responsible for my hypothetical diagnosis.

But what could *they do*? Could they wave a magic wand and simply cure my cancer? No, they could not. Could they suspend the laws of nature and remove the mutation that initiated the tumor? No, they could not. Could they rewind time, and re-route my destiny? No, they could not. No, all of those "supernatural" qualities are simply out of their power. But, would their powerlessness over this situation make them useless to me (powerless?) as my parents?

By no means!

What my parents could do, and what I know they would do, is to be present with me. They would call me. They would visit me. They would support me as I sought the advice of medical professionals. They would provide financial support to sustain my family. They would pray for me, and ask their friends and church members to do likewise. They would be with me—even when they were not present to me, physically. Throughout the process, regardless how deep and dark the valley I had to traverse, they would love me. In short, they would do everything, absolutely everything they *could do* for me. And if my disease were eliminated medically, surgically, they would celebrate with me. If it disappeared, as on a very rare occasion diseases unexplainably do, they would rejoice. And, if the disease won that final battle, they would be heartbroken—but would still be with me, to grieve, and they would remain present for my family who survived my death. Everything…they would do everything they could. And I would know that at every turn, with every angle, in every single thing they would be there for me. But they could not "cure" me, because they simply do not have that power.

Now, as this thought experiment continues, let us ask the really hard question: would I really want them to have this power? (Think carefully before you answer.)

The quick, easy answer, upon which too much theology is based, is: Yes, of course! I would want to be healed, so I would want them to have that power. But, think carefully about what that would mean? What else would it mean, if my parents really did have the power to intervene within the natural process? What would that mean if they could subvert natural order and do, even once, what could not be done? What would it do to my psyche, as a "free" child, a mature, responsible son of theirs, to know that at any moment they could pull down the foundations of the universe and change the immutable laws of nature, just for me? (Or just against me!)

You may still be answering yes, but consider the fact that I have a brother and a sister—and let us further hypothesize that each of them was also tragically diagnosed with a terminal disease. What if my parents chose to heal me but I watched both of my siblings wither away and die long, agonizing deaths—even though my parents actually had the power to heal them? What would that mean to me? What would it mean to my siblings? What would it mean about my parents? Or, what if they chose to heal my sister and brother, and I watched my siblings enjoy the benefits of restored health and wholeness, while I suffered, and finally knew that there was to be no healing. What would that mean?

Isn't that precisely what we say of God and God's power?

What we need to say, precisely, is that God is not The Divine Force, manipulating the laws of nature and human lives capriciously, by a heavenly whim or by a pleading coercion. God is greater than that. God is more powerful. God is more honorable. God is more awe-inspiring. God is more just. God is more mysterious.

Reflecting on the thoughts of the sixteenth-century mystic John of the Cross, James Finley speaks to this understanding of God and love: "Though it is true that there's no refuge from suffering; it's also true that suffering has no refuge from love. Love protects us from nothing, even as it sustains us in all things."[9]

God is love, and love always does all it can do.

So let us learn to say with a religious conviction worthy of our most faithful and disciplined thinking: God always does all that Love can do.

On Needing the Unnecessary God

Psalm 46:1, 10, 11; John 4:21–24

Russ Dean, January 4, 2009

"I do not feel obliged to believe that the same God who has endowed us with sense, reason, and intellect has intended us to forgo their use."[10] So said Galileo Galilei, the seventeenth-century Italian mathematician and physicist who has been called the "father of modern science." Such a conviction, an imperative to *love God with all your mind* (Mark 12:30), is the impetus for today's sermon, which is not an exegesis of either of the texts I have chosen. Nor are my remarks what you may expect to hear from a Baptist pulpit (if you happen to be visiting with us today). This church has a long-held commitment to what it has daringly called an "open pulpit," by which it not only tolerates but actively encourages its pastors to speak their minds freely. (It can be a dangerous policy!) With those as qualifying remarks, I speak to you today from my heart. This may best be regarded something of an autobiographical sermon, reflective of the current state of a journey of faith which is largely predicated upon a firm commitment to two distinct but related disciplines of study. I will return to these commitments in a moment.

It was October 31, 1992, when Pope John Paul II finally officially spoke on behalf of the Roman Catholic Church to vindicate Galileo—who had dared to believe that Copernicus's heretical idea was actually no heresy after all, but was a *fact* the church should learn to live with: the *earth* is not the center of the universe. Imagine that! For championing a heliocentric (sun-centered) theology, Galileo was ordered to stand trial for heresy in 1633 and to spend the rest of his life under house arrest because he would not recant his view. I intend no swipe at the Catholic Church to say 350 years is quite *too long* to come around to the truth! My remark is intended as a critique of dogmatic religion of any persuasion—that is, Roman Catholic, Protestant, or Orthodox practice, or any brand of *any other* religion which finds it necessary to close its eyes to empirical truth in order to defensively adhere to its creeds.

How many times has the church adamantly defended its so-called "truth," even with great injustice perpetrated in its service, only to have to return, hat in hand, at some much-belated hour, to apologize to the world again? How many times? We who are the followers of one who is called *the Way, the Life, the Truth*[11] must never be afraid of truth, however at odds a new revelation may seem with current belief. George Bernard Shaw said, "All great truths begin as blasphemies."[12]

I am ashamed of much of our religious history, littered as it is with its slavish defenses of "eternal dogmas"—which only turned out to be some prejudice or fear or myopia (short-sightedness) ensconced in ecclesial authority and held over the people as a divine bludgeon. If God *is,* then God will always be, and every new glimpse of reality will only serve to enhance our understanding of the divine. It is no mistake that nearly every encounter with the divine recorded in Scripture begins with those simple words: *Fear not.*[13]

The first commitment in my journey of faith is an indelible, undeniable, unavoidable belief in God. Yes, I believe. I believe because my parents taught me to believe. I believe because my church and my school and my mentors and my friends all along my path have nurtured that belief. I believe because my own experience keeps pointing to something which is beyond. Because every commitment I hold as true and every sentiment I feel deep within, every thought I think and every move I make seems to me to brim with the possibility of a great mystery beyond, yet somehow in our midst. As Frank Tupper taught me, I believe in God, because I believe in Jesus. Because in his life, in his death, and in his resurrection, I find a God who is worthy of my life's devotion, a God of sacrificial love, a God who is beyond every conceivable possibility, and always offering new life. And, finally, I believe because I hope.[14]

I believe in God.

The second commitment of my journey is a growing commitment to the truth of science. I will stop short of saying "I believe in science," because "belief" is a word of faith, and science is about what we can see, not what we can believe. I am committed to the truth of science because, well, look up. Do you know that with the touch of one button, one person can electrify this entire room and fill it with light? Isn't that incredible? It took thousands of hours of experimentation and failure for Thomas Edison to show the truth of a theory he had, namely, that you can make light from electricity. It seemed crazy to begin with. No one would have believed it before his discovery in 1879,[15] but there it is, right in front of you—the truth of science. And I am committed to the truth of science because a few weeks ago, in celebration of his tenth birthday, Bennett and I walked into a steel cylinder that weighs several thousand pounds and sat in comfort, completely unamazed by the fact that that steel cylinder, which we call an airplane, raised itself on the wings of Bernoulli's principle, all the way to 30,000 feet above earth's surface, and took us all the way to Boston, Massachusetts, 859 miles, in less than four hours (including a layover in Baltimore!). There it was, right in front of us—the truth of science. And I am committed to the truth of science because this past week, during Christmas, Mary Ryan and Kate Howard sat among the Jacks family to celebrate the birth of a baby named Jesus. Some of you have followed their nine-month trial: Born in March, they did not weigh three pounds between them; they had not one functioning lung among their four; and they were given less than a five percent chance of survival. Nine months later, because of countless hours of medical research, machines that breathe for us, medicines that fight disease for us, and doctors who can operate on the thread-sized intestines of two-pound human beings, Mary Ryan and Kate are thirteen-pound testimonials to the truth of science! There they were—right in front of us—the truth of science.

Yet, at some point, the church tends to draw its line in the sand. The current line for many is the so-called battle between creationism and evolution. I say "so-called" because that battle is over, folks. The lights are still burning! And evolution is no more "just a theory," as some detractors claim, than is the theory of gravity. All the word *theory* means for scientists is that, so far, experimentally, gravity seems to be holding its own. It *is* theoretically possible for it to fail, but until it does, the "theory" of gravity will stand. And so the theory of evolution is not just some fanciful trail of untruth postulated by some anti-religious geeky science-types in a classroom. The theory is the result of empirical (touchable, tasteable, tangible, measurable) *evidence*. In my view, until we are willing to turn out the lights, to deny the empirical truth of electricity, to take back our medications to the pharmacist and say "no thanks," to return our donated organs, and to trust the survival of our children (as Christian Scientists do) *only* to the hand of God—until that day, our integrity will require that we accept science in all its forms—and to learn to live with *God*, with *all* its findings.

I believe in God.

I am committed to the truth of science—*regardless* of where that empirical evidence takes us.

So what do we do when science says God is no longer necessary? We have a few choices—because *that is where we are*. First, we could let such evidence destroy our faith or let it make us deny that such a faith was ever real to begin with. We can let an empirical lack of proof disprove God (even though *God* never makes any claims to be *empirical* at all). Such is the fate of too many *former* believers. Science has taken their God.

The second, maybe most popular choice is to take the position of the church in many of its former battles and to defensively strike back, to deny scientific truth and to engage in a winner-takes-all battle with the scientific establishment. The fundamentalism we are seeing, worldwide, is largely the result of just such a position. It is fearful. Defensive. Insecure. Backward looking. When did this last chapter of American fundamentalism begin? In response to the Scopes trial, which unfortunately put God and Darwin on the stand in 1926, opposing each other. Fundamentalism is attractive because of the confidence that it purports, but it is nearly always wrong in nearly every regard. The future is forward. It always has been. Clinging to our past, and to our ideas built on this past, will never lead us to God.

I think there is a better way. The way forward for believers who are committed to *loving God with all their minds* (Mark 12:30) is to accept the findings of science in every regard—the electricity that makes us comfortable and the disturbing findings that make us uncomfortable. There was a time when God was seen as essential to the universe, because science simply could not explain a universe without a creator. Now it can. One of the famous proofs of the existence of God postulated that the necessary chain of cause and effect, when taken far enough into our past, would have to lead to a first cause. And that cause had to be God. There was simply no other explanation. This makes sense to most of us. It certainly makes sense to me. It seems reasonable, rational. But mathematics, which is the language of science, has now demonstrated through physics that this is not so. I can't explain this science to you, folks (I'm a pastor and not a physicist!), but you don't have to dig into any obscure scientific journal to find that this is *accepted truth* among cosmologists. This world didn't need a "first mover" to start moving.

Given my commitments, then, to God and *then* to science, I've been wondering for some time about this Unnecessary God, wondering if this is a subject I could preach on. After being admittedly rattled by the thought, though, it occurred to me that it's not really the necessary things in life that make life worth living, is it? Take breathing, for example. We can't do without it. It's necessary. But because of the advances of science, there are plenty of human beings today who are breathing, who can hardly be considered living—certainly not living the *abundant life* that Jesus promises (John 10:10). Machines can breathe for us. Only God can fill that wind with a Spirit of life. Conversely, relationships are not, technically, necessary. Though John Donne's truth is spiritually undeniable—"No man is an island"—it is true, technically speaking, that we can survive all alone. Last week Amy and I watched, again, Tom Hanks in his depressing movie *Cast Away*. You *can* survive on a deserted island, all by yourself, eating nothing but coconuts and biding your time. You can. But who wants to?

It seems to me that all the best things in life are really not necessary at all. Life is one thing...eternal life, *abundant living*, an entirely different matter altogether.[16] So I'm willing to grant that God may not be necessary, as the physicists measure necessity, but such a truth makes me no less able to proclaim—it may, in fact, make me more interested in proclaiming the world's need for this Unnecessary God. For, to breathing, God gives spirit. To rules, God gives relationships (that eventually nullify most of the rules!). To all the necessary laws of the universe, both natural and civic, God adds a touch of grace. Who among us could live without grace? And who would want to?

The Roman Catholic theologian Teilhard de Chardin, who was even more committed to science than I, because he actually understood most of it, once said that perhaps humanity needed to find God less in the Alpha and more in the Omega.[17] Less the necessary beginning point of life, and more the destination to which we are moving. Less the biological necessity, and more the spiritual grace—which is where our evolution will take us if we will allow the spirit of God to move among us.[18]

The hope of the church is this: that all the little Jacob Barners we introduce to such a glorious adopted family will truly be allowed, even encouraged, to love God with *all* of their minds.[19] And that the church will give Jacob a God who is big enough and grand enough and mysterious enough, that such a God cannot be chased out of any "bolt holes," that Jacob's God will need no refuge in which to hide.[20] That we will give Jacob a God who is *creative* enough to work with *chance*. Who is *real* enough to be found in *randomness*. Who is *great* enough and *good* enough to transcend any *gaps*, that even when science fills them all, and we should hope it will, there will still be cause to celebrate mystery, and to know it as the divine, among us. Jacob deserves to be given such a God. I'm willing to say, he (and we) needs just such a God.

Richard Dawkins has been one of the most outspoken proponents of a godless universe. You find his skepticism printed in your bulletin. So I was amazed to hear a hint of theological possibility sneak out in a dialogue with Francis Collins, the pioneer of the human genome project, who has ruffled the feathers of some in the scientific world by maintaining rather traditional Christian views. "If there is a God," the famous atheist says, "it's going to be a whole lot bigger and a whole lot more incomprehensible than anything that any theologian of any religion has ever proposed."[21] Dawkins is right. God is bigger and more incomprehensible than the world can ever imagine. But he is wrong to suggest that no theologian has ever before proposed this thought. That God is *just* that big, just that incomprehensible, is why the psalmist, even in his pre-scientific worldview, exhorted his hearers to…*Be still*…for in the mystery of the stillness, and maybe only there, you can…*know that I am God.* And it is why Jesus told the woman at the well that a time is coming

(I am afraid we are still not there yet), but a time is coming when humanity *will* worship God, but neither on "our mountain" nor in "our Jerusalem." Jesus wants us to know that the God who is *Spirit and Truth* will not be worshiped in the comforts of any geography or religious landscape that we can claim to control. The mystery of this world, which we name God, is beyond any location, will not be confined by *any* religious monopoly. When we learn to worship in Spirit and in Truth, we will know God as the *Spirit* within, which, alone, gives that abiding peace. We will know God as the *Spirit* without, which beckons us into relationship with one another. And we will know God as *Truth*, which may be glimpsed, even in an empirical world, but never fully known.

People of God, for little Jacob, let us never be afraid of Truth. And let us learn to celebrate the Unnecessary God who will ever be beyond our control but never fully beyond our reach.

May it be so!

Notes

[1] Alfred North Whitehead, *Adventures of Ideas*, (Glencoe, IL: Free Press, 1967).

[2] Sting, "The Lazarus Heart," *Nothing Like the Sun.* A&M, 1987.

[3] I do not often use this language, as I am convinced faith is not "believing" (i.e., mental assent) as much as it is "trusting," "acting," or "living" based on a particular set of convictions.

[4] Frederick Buechner, *Listening to Your Life* (San Francisco: HarperOne, 1992).

[5] I use the quotation marks as an allusion to Dietrich Bonhoeffer's suggestion that the true God is always a God beyond or above the "God" of even our very best ideas and language.

[6] I actually despise the phrase "spiritual but not religious," but it seems an apt way to characterize those who might use the "God language" of our culture.

[7] The allusion is to the book by Rabbi Lawrence Kushner, *When Bad Things Happen to Good People,* (New York: Random House, Inc., 1981).

[8] I hope it is obvious to the reader that I am being sarcastic and ironic!

[9] Quoted in "Suffering: Week 2 Summary," *Center for Action and Contemplation,* https://cac.org/suffering-week-2-summary-2018-10-27/.

[10] This is one of those quotations that has made it into my files over the years. https://www.goodreads.com/quotes/2388-i-do-not-feel-obliged-to-believe-that-the-same

[11] John 14:6 actually says, "*I am the way, the truth, the life.*" I have reversed the order of the final two nouns for emphasis.

[12] www.goodreads.com/quotes/4670-all-great-truths-begin-as-blasphemies

[13] Though many references might be cited, since we have just completed the Christmas season, I offer only the well-known announcement from the angel to those *shepherds in the field, keeping watch over their flocks by night.... Do not be afraid!* (Luke 2:8–10).

[14] Belief is a complex commitment. In this paragraph I have tried to be honest about my reasons for belief and to acknowledge that believing in God has been, given my particular life,

largely culturally conditioned. A Baptist minister's son, raised in the South, in the twentieth century, could hardly believe otherwise! Yet not only my raising but my own personal experience and my own intellectual search have contributed to my belief (which is now mine and not just my parents' or my culture's belief). And believing amounts to hope. I do believe in God, at least in part, because I hope there is God. *And hope will not disappoint us* (Rom 5:5).

[15] My quick refresher course on the internet on Edison's most famous discovery led me to the Wikipedia reference, which indicated that the incandescent bulb had actually been discovered before Edison, who simply refined and perfected the filament. The article did not cite the original inventor. See the Wikipedia entry for Thomas Edison: https://en.wikipedia.org/wiki/Thomas_Edison.

[16] Someone commented that the reference to "eternal life" was distracting to them. In the midst of this sermon, to be asked to think about the afterlife, heaven, took them, momentarily, down a different road. I responded, "So who said anything about heaven, the afterlife?" Though the critique is probably right, and certainly understandable, "eternal life," as I understand it (and I believe I can make a biblical case for this position), is equivalent to "abundant living"—it is the life that "God desires" for us, a life that begins now and (as our blessed hope), we believe, continues even beyond this life. But the point is the living now, full, free, abundant. My friend Dr. Bill Hull taught me that "eternal" need not mean "endless time," or quantity of life (as we most often conceive of heaven, i.e., "forever"), but may very well indicate fullness in depth or quality of life. The Greek word *kairos*, which means "time" (but is distinct from the word chromos, which counts time, as in a *chronograph*, a clock), indicates that every moment holds the possibility of being an "eternal moment," shot through with all the purpose and meaning of God. Every single moment.

[17] This quotation comes to me in Robert Wright's book *Nonzero* as a quotation of a paraphrase from an unnamed source! "(One theologian has paraphrased Teilhard as belief that "God must become for us less Alpha than Omega.)" Robert Wright, *Nonzero: The Logic of Human Destiny*, (New York: Pantheon Books, 1999), 332.

[18] I believe God can take us beyond our biologically driven evolution (perhaps this is the purpose of such an "unnecessary God"). Rather than simply following the dictates of our "selfish genes" (a phrase common to Darwinians), God calls us beyond the biological drive, to the accomplishments of self-less love, of self-giving, self-sacrifice, and partnership. At what point would any "selfish gene" call us *to love our enemy* (Matt 5:44); *to lay down [our] life for our friend* (John 15:13)?

[19] There was a parent/child dedication service for Jacob earlier in our worship.

[20] "Darwin chased God out of his old haunts in biology, and he scurried for safety down the rabbit hole of physics. The laws and constants of the universe, we were told, are too good to be true: a setup, carefully timed to allow the eventual evolution of life. It needed a good physicist to show us the fallacy, and Victor Stengel lucidly does so. The faithful won't change their minds, of course (that is what faith means), but Victor Stengel drives a pack of energetic ferrets down the last major bolt hole and God is running out of refuges in which to hide." Richard Dawkins, in a book-jacket review of Victor Stengel's *God, The Failed Hypothesis* (Buffalo, NY: Prometheus Books, 2007).

[21] "When we started out and we were talking about the origins of the universe and the physical constants, I provided what I thought were cogent arguments against a supernatural intelligent designer. But it does seem to me to be a worthy idea. Refutable—but nevertheless grand and big enough to be worthy of respect…. [Traditional religious ideas] strike me as parochial. If there is a God, it's going to be a whole lot bigger and a whole lot more incomprehensible than

anything that any theologian of any religion has ever proposed." Richard Dawkins in a *Time* magazine debate with Francis Collins: David Van Biema, "God vs. Science," *Time Magazine*, (Sunday, Nov. 05, 2006) http://content.time.com/time/magazine/article/0,9171,1555132-9,00. html.

A New Devotion: Never Forget the Importance of Disciplined Thinking

Questions to Consider

How do you grow in faith?

Have you ever really studied your religion? Your faith? Your Bible?

When you read, do you look for books and topics and authors who affirm what you already believe? What about sources of news? Social media platforms? When you go to church, do you expect classes and worship to reinforce what you already believe or to challenge you?

How important is theology (the "study of God") to you? How important is it to the work of the church in the world? Is it "ivory tower" gibberish, or is it really important?

What is the difference between knowledge and wisdom? Is growing in faith about increasing knowledge or wisdom or both?

If we simplified our world of quantum physics and technology and digital communication to a level that the average person could understand, would our complex world continue to function? Doesn't someone need to understand the mind-numbing detail? How does this relate to matters of faith?

We think of *theology* as "the study of God," but the word comes from two Greek stems, *God* and *word* (or logic, *logos*). Rather than suggesting definitive answers or explanations, how would it change your growth in faith if your theology freed you to "explore God" rather than "explain God"?

Write a free association of words that come to mind when you think of "God."

❖

The first of the four cardinal virtues of the Roman Catholic Church is "prudentia," which basically means damn good thinking. Christ came to take away our sins, not our minds.
—William Sloane Coffin[1]

For a kid who had asked a zillion questions about a zillion things, I had lived a surprisingly calm and confident adolescence. The urge to sprout wings and fly (fueled by juvenile happiness), the need to cut ties and run (energized by pubescent hormones) had evaded my soul. I had the answers about the important stuff. There were no existential ghosts haunting me, no horizons calling me to reject my roots, rebel from my raising, rewrite my own religion. A renegade I was not. Any rebelling I've done came after I became a pastor!

College *had* opened the door to the questions, however, and I was still reeling, sensing that there was (perhaps?) a new world on the other side of my "Blessed One-Time-I-Had-Assurance." At this state, though, I had not found my way. Looking back, it's safe to say that at this point along the journey, I didn't even know what I didn't know.

In search of theological peace, we drove into Louisville, Kentucky, one late-summer day in 1988. My little Mazda B2000 was loaded to the gills, all our worldly possessions compression-fitted under the truck topper that covered the bed of my burgundy and white pickup. I was anxious to enroll at the Southern Baptist Theological Seminary, and Amy had secured a job teaching first grade at an interesting private school located in a suburb called Shively. Louisville's more affluent residents sometimes condescended that impoverished community as "Lively Shively."

Amy's church background had been similar to mine, and though she was an elementary education major at Presbyterian College (PC), a fine, small liberal arts college in our hometown, Clinton, South Carolina, she had minored in religion. A handful of undergraduate religion courses, taught mostly by ordained Presbyterian ministers with academic credentials, had rocked her world only slightly less than a full major in religion had fully rocked mine. PC, which is affiliated with the more progressive branch of the Presbyterian family tree (Presbyterian Church [USA]), had garnered a similar reputation to my Baptist alma mater, with good Christian students in both institutions being consistently warned by conservative pastors to guard with caution against the "liberal religion faculty" who will "take away your faith" if you're not careful.

Because she had an interest in learning about the Christian education degree offered at Southern, and in order not to be isolated from my new world of friends and study, Amy had signed up to take one course that fall. That Monday night introduction to seminary life changed her trajectory in teaching and bound us together in a theological fate that neither of us had imagined. If you can endure a metaphor in Einsteinian galactic conjecture, it seems we were both positioned on the edge of the same wormhole, and the stars and forces and energies all aligned as we entered the mother home of all Southern Baptist seminaries. Almost immediately we were swept headlong through a black hole of questioning and doubting and out the other side into a beautiful, infinite world of new possibilities. If that space did not provide new answers, it gave us an atmosphere that let us breathe freely in the questions.

Back home, however, the new world we were experiencing didn't seem so life-giving. We sent regular messages home, and I suppose those reports to parents and siblings conveyed the enthusiasm we were finding in that path of doubts and discoveries. I was like a kid again, again asking a zillion questions, and again wanting to share all my knowledge with anyone who would listen, and even to some who weren't so interested! Apparently they got the message.

We are close to both sides of the in-laws divide, and both families have always done a good job of staying in touch and visiting those few who have strayed from Laurens County. Over our seminary years we entertained parents, siblings, our young nieces and nephews in a schedule of consistent-enough-not-to-be-forgotten contacts from home. Still in our first year, still wet behind the ears with newness and excitement, we had a visit. I don't remember the specific guests, but I do remember stopping as we walked through Broadus Lounge, the student lounge located in Norton Hall. As we chatted there, one of our family members said something like, "It's great that you're enjoying your classes so much. It's good to study and learn—and you obviously have to give the professors what they want on exams—but don't let them really change what you *really* believe!"

Maybe that's what a lot of church people expect out of their students who've experienced a call to ministry, gone off to school excited about faith and learning: "Go get all the education you can—just don't let them change what you really think!" But what kind of minister would that make you? And why waste the time to begin with if you're only going to parrot professors for passing grades but return to churches who want to believe nothing but what they've always believed?

The American philosopher and psychologist William James noted "A great many people think they are thinking when they are merely rearranging their prejudices."[2] My education did not rearrange my prejudices; it exploded them with awareness and analysis, giving me a new way to think—not just new thoughts about old, unchanged ideas.

There is a difference in indoctrination—which just rearranges our preju-dices to enforce them all over again—and education—which opens the door, unafraid, to a free and unimpeded exploration of the questions. Much of the church practices indoctrination. That is what was expected of us, as commu-nicated by one of our well-meaning family members. I'm grateful to have been exposed, instead, to the methodology of education. I understand that this is an anxious prospect: What if they come back believing…differently? What if they actually…change? Yes, indoctrination would be easier, more comfortable, for teachers and students alike, but there is no way forward without education.

Before she became the president of Central Baptist Theological Seminary, Dr. Molly Marshall was a professor of systematic theology at the Southern Baptist Theological Seminary. She insisted that all her students call her by her first name, and Amy and I had both been in Molly's classes at Southern. Her impact on us still runs deep. After we had been on staff at Clemson's First Baptist Church for two years, church leaders approached us with an invitation to become ordained by that community of faith. They gave us the opportunity to plan our service of ordination, and there was never a moment's question who would preach that sermon.

Molly's passion for scholarship was rigorous. Her devotion to Christian faith was inspiring. Her love for students was legendary. And her effect on real lives was practical—Molly changed our living by changing our thinking. After she preached in a morning service of worship on the date of All Hallows Eve, 1993, Molly knelt before me, grasped my hands, and looked me dead in the eye as she said, "Russ, never forget the importance of disciplined thinking."

When Molly knelt before me during that ancient, holy practice the church calls "the laying on of hands," her touch and her sincerity and her challenge rang true to the life she had shown me in the classroom. Her call has never left me. The call to a devotional and professional life of disciplined thinking has left an indelible mark on teaching and preaching, in personal reflection and reading for pleasure. Because of Molly's ongoing influence, with "disciplined thinking" imprinted on my soul, I have come to believe that the gospel is too powerful, Scripture's truths too complex, and the religious life too filled with deep, rich potential to ever want to dumb down a message or waste a teaching opportunity with the sentimental saccharine of "chicken soup for the spiritual soul" or with what one pastor has called "sweet Jesus" sermons.

I am aware that there is a pastoral liability inherent in the responsibility Molly entrusted to me, and it is the danger of trying to communicate too much, too often, of offering messages that are too deep or too broad to be easily encapsulated into the sound bites that our culture demands, diseased as it is with attention deficit disorder. I readily admit this, as readily as I admit that I have no idea how to solve the problem! There is a fine line between making any of the messages of the Bible's challenges easily understood (as spiritually and socially and politically charged as they are)—and in so watering down transcendent, transformational truth that the deep, inherent challenge is lost.

Writing to a friend in 1799, the poet William Blake said, "You say that I want somebody to Elucidate my Ideas. But you ought to know that What is Grand is necessarily obscure to Weak men. That which can be made Explicit to the Idiot is not worth my care. The wisest of the Ancients consider'd what is not too Explicit as the fittest for Instruction, because it rouzes the faculties to act."[3]

To be clear, I do not think of my congregation as filled with "weak men," as Blake's patriarchal language may suggest. Quite the contrary, and I refer again to the experience I share in my sermon "On Controlling the Faithful" (chap. 4). I asked a friend and trusted mentor, an experienced pastor, "Can you be honest about your doubts and concerns and share them openly with your congregation?" His answer shocked me: "You can never be fully honest [with your congregation] about what you believe."

Wow. Really? Why not? Can I not trust a *community* of faith with my honesty? Is that because I do not value their intelligence or because they will not value mine? Will I actually honor faith, theirs or mine, by being anything less than forthright about my experiences, my joys, my doubts?

At that moment I made a promise to myself that if I ever became a pastor, I would never not be honest. I have held true to that promise for more than seventeen years. My congregation knows that if they do not want to know what I really think about a scripture or about the virgin birth or about the last decision by the Supreme Court...do not ask! I trust the intelligence of my congregation, many of whom are unquestionably smarter than I. I know they have experienced many of those issues in life than can lead to a crisis of faith, and I know they are strong enough to hold their ground even when they disagree with their pastor. I actually believe regular old church people are even smart enough to understand historical-critical methodology, dispensational pre-millennialism, and apocalyptic eschatology!

Now, I do understand that not everyone is equally drawn to theological concepts and inquiry, that most people in the pews have not had formal education in religion and theology, and that the particular lexicon of any particular discipline of study may sound foreign or pedantic just out of unfamiliarity. I have also been reminded by a parishioner's critique that "after a long week in the office, I just don't want to come to church and have to work that hard."

I get it. I really do.

It's just that I'm not sure how you "get it" (important, timely, needed, often-unconventional spiritual truth) if you're not willing to work that hard! So often we have had people say, "I really want to know more about the Bible," but the honest truth is that they really do not. Most people can't even make the time in their busy schedules to read the Bible—much less to study it. The title of a book by the former megachurch pastor and New York Times bestselling author Rob Bell is instructive: *What Is the Bible? How an Ancient Library of Poems, Letters, and Stories Can Transform the Way You Think and Feel About Everything.* That says it all.

The Bible is not a book. It's a library. It was not written in our English vernacular, and its setting doesn't reflect our culture. It's filled with poetry—and you know how many people hate poems. Much of the content of the New Testament is in the form of letters written to one of the early churches from its founding pastor—and it is not always obvious why they were written and to whom, specifically, so the point is not always so easy to understand. And stories are wonderful, but they are notoriously multilayered and filled with nuance and analogy and metaphor and cryptic symbolism. Yes, the Bible *can* "transform the way you think and feel about *everything*"—but only if you really understand it.

Understand?

In that one sentence she spoke in that holy moment, Molly Marshall blessed and cursed me—for a lifetime! So you might understand how the one bumper sticker I've ever been willing to display has become my motto for ministry. I used the paradoxical humor as a sermon title once, and the next week a church member showed up with a gift. It says, simply, "Eschew Obfuscation."

That's perfect!

Avoid making things difficult to understand. Yes, of course. How else will anyone ever go away from a sermon or lesson with any nugget of truth that can actually change them? I don't want to waste people's time. This is my profession—*my calling*. I want people to understand, be inspired, leave renewed. I really do.

I just want to teach it right, though, and I'm convinced that much (most?) Bible teaching so simplifies the message, making most of the stories into simple moralistic tales and most of the truths into hardened dogmatic rules, that the rich literary character of the Bible, with its invitation to probe life's deepest questions, is lost to simple, literal answers.

I'm grateful for Dr. Molly Marshall. I'm grateful for her life and for her influence and for her challenge that truly ordained me to a lifetime of devotion in study and serious reflection. We live in the age of quantum mechanics and artificial intelligence. It should be more than clear that reality is too complex to be made simple—and spiritual truth, the transcendent power that can offer meaning and purpose to human beings in every age, is deep, rich, multilayered—and it is invitational, begging us to join the journey of personal exploration.

Finding spiritual truth is hard work—but when we are willing to engage in that work, we will find the truth—and the work—so much more fulfilling than settling for simple answers.

Eschew Obfuscation (But the Gospel Really Is Too Big to Fit in a Nutshell!)

OR *On Being "Born Again": Difficult Truth, the Risk of Reductionism, and the Not-Simple Power of Good News*

OR *God So Loved the Word... (And That's All I've Got to Say About That)*

John 3:1–21

Russ Dean, July 3, 2011 (Summer Series: A Testimony of Texts: Part 3)

Sometimes a title just says it all. And if I have to say so myself, I think I nailed it with today's sermon title. Don't you!? And it's one sermon title, not three. It's not like you can just choose the one you like the best. For Amy and me, finding just the right title is important. It really does guide our thinking, the direction of the sermon as we are writing, and I was so proud when this one just came to me. Ah…there it is, I thought. All they'll have to do is just read the title, and they'll understand the whole sermon. It's just that simple.

"Eschew Obfuscation"—probably my favorite, all-time bumper sticker. It inspired me to write a children's song for Camp Prism by the same title. I'll sing it for you sometime. But not now—I've got too much to say. Eschew obfuscation—you know, avoid making things difficult! That's what it's all about, right? Especially from the pulpit. Like the homiletics strategy of one old preacher who said there are three components to a good sermon: "1. Tell 'em what you're gonna tell 'em. 2. Tell 'em. 3. Tell 'em what you told 'em." I really wish preaching were that simple. Some of you wish that too![4]

And for many folks the sermon is just that simple, especially when it comes to a "simple verse" like John 3:16. The story sounds something like this (if you'll allow me a little pastoral/poetic license): Jesus had been sitting around in heaven, since he and God created Alpha Centauri and the Big Dipper and the Grand Canyon and Mt. Everest and all those dinosaur fossils (which they threw in just to confound the paleontologists!). Jesus had been biding his time, you see, until God sent him down to straighten things out, because human beings had made a real mess of our situation. He sort of just fell through Mary's womb on his way to human adulthood, wandering around Galilee about thirty years, again, biding his time until it was time for the cross.[5] Which is the only reason he came to begin with. God sent him here to die, because that's the only way you can go to heaven, which is, of course, the only point of life. Those are the rules, you see; God made them up. God loves you so much that someone has to die in order for you to be saved. That's the rule. And don't ask why God didn't just change the rule, since God is in charge of everything, especially the rules, because we're not supposed to ask. That's just the way it is. So Jesus did his part, as required by the rule, but you still have to do your part, which is to believe the right things about Jesus, and if you do, then you're in, but if you don't, then…well, sorry, whether you lived eighty-five good years or just thirteen miserable ones, if you didn't believe the right things about Jesus and pray the right prayer, then, well…you're going to hell when you die, and it's going to be a long, miserable eternity.

And that's the way it is. Because God loves you just that much.

I've got to pause here and say, please stay with me, and please don't take offense at my sarcasm. I'm not disparaging our scripture. I've told you over and over how much I love it and how important I think it still is for modern Christians. And I'm not making fun of anyone else's theology. I am not. But

I am trying to put in stark terms the story as many of us learned it, because I think the way it is often taught does no justice to the depth and beauty of a gospel story that really is about a love that is universal, whose reach extends an entire infinite cosmos.

It's been called the "gospel in a nutshell" because it is, according to a certain reading, easy enough even for a child to understand on face value. In fact, we hardly even have to quote the verse—apparently just showing up in the end zone of a televised football game or behind one goal in a basketball arena wearing a multicolored clown wig and holding a poster that simply says "John 3:16"…that's enough. Show up enough. Burn the reference in someone's brain. So somewhere, somehow, someday they will find a Bible and read the verse, and presto…one person has all the information she needs. It's her ticket to heaven. Unless, of course, she reads it and actually understands it on face value, but, for whatever reason (and there could be lots of reasons), rejects it. In this case, your stealth evangelism has just resulted in the opposite effect because the rejection of a simple truth this person didn't even know five minutes before she read the verse has now consigned her poor soul to eternal torment. Forever. She read. She understood. She didn't believe. She'll go to hell. It's as simple as that.

Is it? Is it really just that simple?

The simple point of today's not-so-simple sermon is that any truth that really is big enough to save the whole universe is far too big to be dumbed down into any size nutshell. Sin and salvation and grace and faith and heaven and hell and eternity, birth and new birth and death and resurrection—all of which *are* addressed in this powerful, important verse of Scripture—are too important and too rich and too deep to be cut short, reduced to a simplistic formula for salvation.

This week I spent two days with the nineteen North Carolina pastors I will travel to Israel with later this month. As we were sharing our stories, our lives, our backgrounds, our denominational identities, the conversation inevitably turned to the troubles that have roiled every one of our denominations (a result, no doubt, in every case of reducing complex issues of faith to platitudes and dogmas that are far too small for the God they are supposed to represent, but I digress). A Lutheran pastor was explaining where his church fit in to the landscape of American Lutheranism, and he told of one faction of his chosen denomination whose conservative practice includes closed communion. Visitors and family members are routinely asked to leave—even he, an ordained Evangelical Lutheran pastor, would not be allowed to share communion in this Lutheran church, because he is not a member of that particular church ("Welcome to our church." But not really!).

The pastor of that church also, *incredibly*, refuses to offer communion to a member of his own congregation because she suffers from Down Syndrome—a state which renders her intellectually incapable of "fully understanding what she is doing." So she cannot receive communion. If this logic holds for communion, it surely holds for salvation. In this case, however, her ignorance would *be* her salvation—of course a loving God would not consign to hell someone who could *not* even *understand.* But let us follow this theology to its logical conclusion. Let's assume (just for the sake of this argument) that the actual IQ level required to attain such an understanding is 68. (And if salvation is dependent upon hearing and understanding so you can "accept Christ," there has to be some IQ level at which this is possible—and some level below which one could not be held accountable.) Anyone whose IQ remains at or below that level is safe, for eternity—protected by the mercy of God. But if your IQ is 140…or 97…or suppose it's just 69…well, congratulations, that one IQ point might just cost you your soul. For a very long time.

I am trying to be dramatic. Trying to be a little offensive, let me admit. Because I believe any theology that is shallow enough to deny full community to any faithful, churchgoing, God-loving woman—especially one with a mental handicap. Any such theology is offensive. So is a theology that arrogantly suggests it can adequately summarize the infinite love of God in one sentence. So is a theology that seeks to package the Mystery of Grace in a one-size-fits-all nutshell of soul-saving certainty.

It's just not that simple. (End of sermon.)

I'm reading *Love Wins*—which is the new book by Rob Bell that is apparently shaking the evangelical world with its unorthodox message about "heaven, hell, and the fate of every person who ever lived."[6] Bell is a forty-year-old pastor, a graduate of Wheaton College (that excellent academic institution that prides itself in being something of an evangelical Princeton). Bell founded and has grown Mars Hill Bible Church in Grandville, Michigan, to more than 10,000 members. They meet in a shopping mall which someone gave the church some years ago. He is one of the stars of the megachurch movement, one of those Bible-believing evangelicals who walks around on the stage wearing a portable headset microphone teaching the Bible. You've seen those guys. Many of them are great at what they do. They boil down the truth of Scripture into bite-size nuggets of easy-to-understand, practical, make-my-life-better-today wisdom.

But in *Love Wins*, Bell says we've gotten it wrong. That the story we've heard about heaven and hell is all wrong. All wrong. His book is easy to read. But it's not simple. I've read a hundred pages and he's already quoted 150 Bible verses—most of them to show us how we've misread. I think Bell would agree with the way I told my opening story, even its sarcasm. I know he would agree with today's thesis, that we've made it all too simple—and have missed much of the point in the process.

In his chapter on hell he talks about the story of the rich man and Lazarus from Luke 16. This text is often quoted as proof of the physical existence of a fiery hell where the lost will spend eternity. The rich man dies, and Jesus says he goes to Hades (which is not really hell at all, but I don't have time to explain that here…read the book for yourself![7]), where Jesus says he is in *agony in this fire*. As Bell explains all of this, he makes the following comments:

[The rich man] is alive in death, but in profound torment, because he's living with the reality of not properly dying the kind of death that actually leads a person into the only kind of life that's worth living.

He says, "a pause, to recover from that last sentence." And then he continues.

How do you communicate a truth that complex and a multilayered? You tell a nuanced, shocking story about a rich man and a poor man, and you throw in gruesome details about dogs licking his sores, and then you tell about a massive reversal in their deaths in which the rich man in hell has the ability to converse with Abraham, the father of the faith. And then you end it all with a twist about resurrection, a twist that is actually a hint about something about to happen in real history soon after this parable is told.

Brilliant, just brilliant. There's more…[8]

Do you understand? Bell says that the truth of heaven and hell and God's love is too complex and multilayered and rich and personal for Jesus to have taught it to his disciples in some long, logical lecture about theology—because it is truth about spiritual matters, not literal ones. So Jesus tells a story. And he expects his hearers to realize that it is a story. To hear it as a story. And to know that stories are the best way to speak of spiritual truth—because spiritual truth does not need to be defined—because it cannot be defined with dogmatic certainty. If we could measure God's love, we would need no faith to believe in it. And if we could videotape salvation, we would not need hearts and minds and souls in order to experience it.

The story of Nicodemus is just like that, told by the Bible's most theological, most symbolic, most sophisticated literary gospel writer. It's a story. Please let the story stand. Read it. Experience it. Hear it. And let it speak to you between the lines—because though stories do have to be written with pen and ink, their truth is *never* black and white. Truth speaks to us in all the space and all the silence and all the questions that come when we reflect on a good story.[9]

So Nicodemus comes to Jesus at night. John doesn't mean it was after sundown. He means that Nicodemus was in the dark! And he asks questions like many people ask, which makes it clear to Jesus that he simply doesn't get it. He thinks being *born again* is a physical thing, a literal thing that happens to you one day. Poof, you're *born again*. Wrong again.

I cannot find a commentary that will tell me, simply, that the truth of John 3:16 is as I was taught it as a child. They don't just say that this means if you don't believe in Jesus you're going to hell. It's just more complex than that. And when I asked for feedback from a group of my friends, the response was, likewise, all but simplistic. Dr. James Strange, now on the religion faculty as professor of New Testament at Samford University, said, "You want me to comment on John 3:16 in an email? Holy kamoli!" And then he said this, which sounds a little like all the other commentaries I read:

> Many Christians stress the second part—*so that everyone who believes in him may not perish but may have eternal life*—at the expense of the first: *God so loved the* world. Present-day Christians may focus on the idea that God saves them as individuals but miss the fact that God's love aims at the salvation of the entire world. In the Gospel of John, Jesus tells Nicodemus that God's love is universal: it reaches beyond Jerusalem, Palestine, and even the edges of the Roman Empire. The Samaritans realize this truth when Jesus comes to them (4:42). Alabama Christians do well to remember that this love is neither kept out by the mosque's door nor kept in by the U.S. border.

God's love is universal. For all. Love wins.

So here's what I want our children to know about John 3:16. It's pretty simple: I want you to know John 3:16. If you haven't memorized it, you have homework. Can you say it with me? *For God so loved the world that he gave his only begotten son, that whosoever believeth in him should not perish, but have everlasting life.* And I want you to remember that the most important thing is the first phrase: God so loved the *world*.

I want our youth to understand that Jesus is this *only begotten son* that the gospel talks about—and what that means is that if you want to understand the universal, unconditional, cosmic-reaching love of God…you need to know Jesus. He invites you to follow him. I hope you will.

And I want our adults to understand that a little humility goes a long way. What *does* John 3:16 mean? I don't know. I don't think we're supposed to know, fully. It's one of those great texts that should stay with us for a lifetime. Give us pause. Make us think. And rethink. It is about a love which will never let us go. A love which John calls "cosmic."[10] And it is about Jesus, who taught us that love in life, in death, in resurrection. And it is a story by the church, because it is a story about the church—the church of the feeble, frail, trying-to-understand-but-willing-to-follow-anyway followers of one who calls us to everlasting life.

For God so loved the world that he gave his only begotten son, that whosoever believeth in him should not perish, but have everlasting life.

Everlasting *life…*

Everlasting life…

Even today.

May it be so!

Notes

[1] William Sloane Coffin, *Credo*, (Louisville, KY: Westminster John Knox Press, 2004), 8.

[2] I do not have a citation for this quotation. A search engine called "quoteinvestigator.com" says: "The earliest close match known to QI appeared in 1906 in the religious periodical 'Zion's Herald' based in Boston, Massachusetts…. 'Bishop Oldham scored with his audience with a bon mot to the effect that some people "think they are thinking when they are merely rearranging their prejudices.'… Knute Rockne used the expression in a newspaper column in 1926, but he disclaimed credit. William James received credit by 1946, and he did write a thematically similar passage in 1907 before his death in 1910. Yet, QI has found no direct evidence that James made a closely matching statement. Edward R. Murrow received credit by 1949, and he may have used it after it had been circulating for years."

³ This is one of those "brainy quotes" gleaned from the internet. The citation reads: William Blake, Letter to Dr. Trusler, 23 August 1799.

⁴ I found this a very interesting sermon to write and preach because the sermon itself is a bit of a metaphor for the constant battle with preaching that I face, especially at PRBC. My preaching has always been "heady"—I am not an intellectual, but I am certainly idea-oriented, and this comes through in the themes I choose and the way I approach most texts—looking for an idea, a theological concept with which I can grapple. (This is a contrast to the "hearty" or situation-oriented way that Amy approaches the pulpit.) PRBC has consistently said to us that they want us to grapple with the issues—and to challenge them to do so. And it is the "hard sermons" that I get the most affirmation for preaching—yet those sermons undoubtedly speak to a narrow audience within the congregation. The more I preach to my own strength, then, the more I feel distanced to a segment of the congregation. It is a conundrum that I don't know how to solve. I'm convinced that preachers should not "dumb down" the message—but preaching hard texts, dealing with difficult issues, in simple words is quite a challenge.

⁵ I've actually heard Christians who believe that little baby Jesus lay there, consciously aware that in thirty years he would face the cross ("He was God, after all!"). The next thirty years were just a scripted time-killer as he awaited his only purpose for being: the cross.

⁶ Rob Bell, *Love Wins: A Book About Heaven, Hell, and the Fate of Every Person Who Ever Lived* (New York: HarperCollins Publishers, 2011).

⁷ *Hades* is the Greek word that refers to the Jewish concept of the "abode of the dead"—a shadowy place that was the home of all the dead. (The Jews did not have a developed belief in heaven and hell.) *Hades* is not "hell." (Hell derives its name from the Greek word for a Valley of Hinnom just outside of ancient Jerusalem, also called Gehenna, which was the city's garbage dump. Gehenna was a nasty place, where animals roamed, where fires smoldered, where the stench of trash and decay was always in the air. When Jesus refers to *hell*, he is referring to this image.)

⁸ Rob Bell, *Love Wins: A Book About Heaven, Hell, and the Fate of Every Person Who Ever Lived* (New York: HarperCollins Publishers, 2011), 77.

⁹ In the *New Interpreter's Bible* commentary, Gail R. O'Day says, "The very richness of the text complicates the task of the interpreter. There is a temptation to pare down John 3:1–21 to its 'basic' elements—that is, either to summarize its story line (a Jewish religious authority comes to question Jesus) or its lesson (Jesus teaches about faith and judgment). Such summaries are easier to handle than the intricate dialogue and discourse of the text…. The interpreter needs to resist the temptation to distill this text to its essence or paraphrase its substance, however, because to do so does violence to [John's] way of storytelling and risks losing the text's proclamation of the good news." Gail R. O'Day, "John" *The New Interpreter's Bible*, (Nashville, TN: Abingdon Press, 2003), 553-554.

¹⁰ The Greek word is actually *kosmon*, which seems particularly relevant today, with all the advancing knowledge of cosmologists and our growing understanding of our finitely small place in an infinite cosmos!

A New Religion: Everything That's True about Christianity Is a Myth

Questions to Consider

When did you learn about Santa Claus, and when did you learn about God? Do you still believe in Santa? Do you still believe in God? How might your transformation of understanding of one inform your understanding of the other?

What do you regard as "true," and how do you know something is true?

How reliable are facts? Is eyewitness testimony reliable?

How well do you remember the facts of your childhood? When you gather with family members, do you remember events the same way? If not, do these discrepancies in fact change the essential meaning of the event(s) for you?

Is there anything you trust or believe in that is not, strictly speaking, factual?

Are there any stories in the Bible that may not be "literally true" but still convey ultimate truth?

What is your favorite story? What can you learn from this story about what is happening in the world and in your own life? Is that actually what the story is about in the first place?

What role have stories played in your education (what is true, what is real, what is meaningful)?

Tony Campolo, a well-known evangelical who is a great storyteller and a challenging speaker, once said if he found out that there were no heaven or no hell, he would still be a Christian because the Way of Jesus makes sense. How do you react to Campolo's claim?

What aspects of faith can you prove (God, Jesus, the Spirit, miracles, prayer)? If you cannot prove one or more of these aspects, do you still believe? Why or why not?

❖

The final belief is to believe in a fiction, which you know to be a fiction,
there being nothing else. The exquisite truth is to know that it is a fiction
and that you believe in it willingly.
—Wallace Stephens[1]

Charlie Milford was unique. Yes, I know, technically speaking, everyone is unique. So I know that it distorts the literal meaning of the word, but if you knew Charlie, you know what I mean in saying he was uniquely unique! There are those rare individuals who stand out through rare ability or seren-dipitous opportunity or unique charisma—and Charlie was one of those. I have never met a person with a stronger personality. For good, and sometimes for ill, Charlie Milford had the strongest, most rarified persona I have ever encountered.

Charlie had strong opinions. And his were always right.

Charlie had internal courage. And he spoke and acted on those opinions.

Charlie had a sonorous voice. And he was not afraid to use it in speaking truth to power.

Charlie had dynamic leadership. And he led, with never a hint of self-doubt or timidity.

He tells the following story to be true (and it sounds just confidently pious enough not to be doubted!): In 1951 the Park Road Baptist Church in Charlotte, North Carolina, called Charles O. Milford to become the found-ing pastor of a new Southern Baptist congregation that would eventually be planted in the pasture of a dairy farm on the outskirts of a bustling city. Within a year the new pastor penned his own letter of resignation—and dated it 1983. When that year rolled around, three decades hence, he retrieved the letter from his filing cabinet and submitted it to the chairman of the Board of Deacons.

Enough said.

When that same church called Russ and Amy Jacks Dean to become their fifth pastor (co-pastors) in 2000, Charlie Milford could be found sitting in the sanctuary. Every Sunday. While his connection to the church had been held at a distance by his relationship with the intervening three pastors, there was something right about the chemistry between us. Charlie liked the young couple. We were, in turn, enthused by Charlie's friendship, respectful of his position, grateful for his support, and in time became influenced by his opin-ions and courage, by his voice, and by his leadership.

Charlie was sincere in his complementary support, though we would receive the occasional email that began, "Dearly Beloved, I forgive you, but…" (this is also a true story!). Charlie would then go on to carefully enumerate the venal or mortal sins we had committed in the prior week's service of worship, detail why the grievances were so heinous, and then he would end, always, "I love you. Charlie." While we did not always agree with Charlie's judgments, we never had to wonder where he stood, and we never had to doubt his love for us. What's not to like about that?

Charlie had been away from "his church" for a good many years, but when the years had weathered him, he decided to return from the mountain house he had built in his spare time during those pastoral years, buy into one of the local retirement communities, and settle in for the homestretch. I'm not sure when we first made this observation, consciously, but fairly early in the five years we had together, we realized that whether he knew it consciously or not, Charlie had wanted to "come home" to die, and for our part we wanted to be able to be his pastors while at the same time giving him back "his church."

The timing was right. The personalities were compatible. The coincidences might have been providential.

Charlie trained us without overstepping, supported us without (much!) patronizing, modeled leadership without drawing attention, and Charlie taught us. This is just who he was. He *had* moderated his temperament since his pastoral years, but the persona in Charlie was hard to bridle. A leader has to lead; a teacher has to teach.

Way back in the glory years, the progressive Baptist pastors in town (they were a small handful!) had formed a discussion group they called, with more than a touch of irony, "The Humility Club." Charlie had struck up a friendship with Carlyle Marney, the iconic pastor of Myers Park Baptist, and they were the ringleaders. Weekly, the rebels met over lunch for a no-holds-barred free-for-all, a setting that gave them free license to proclaim every new unorthodoxy to their hearts' content, to question any authority, to glory in jettisoning one after another of the old hymns—and the theologies that accompanied them.

The group met for years and had been influential in Charlie's "liberation," which began in earnest when a Sunday school class invited their pastor to conduct a study on the biblical view of hell. After a careful study led him to announce "Eternal damnation is a lie," many of the other evangelical foundations crumbled in rapid succession. At some point along the way, in some

Baptist meeting along the way, some critic who had come to understand Charlie's credo along the way mocked him as "nothing but a Reformed Jew."

Having denied hell and Trinitarian theology and the divinity of Jesus, having demythologized the so-called miracles out of any historical substance, there was some legitimacy to his critic's view—but say what you will of his doctrinal positions, Charlie Milford's commitment to the way of Jesus never wavered. Charlie always prayed "in Jesus's name," and his prayer echoed his convictions to work for the poor in Jesus's name, to voice the failures of justice in Jesus's name, to strive for godliness in Jesus's name, to live with no hesitation the life he thought best underscored faith in Jesus's name.

I don't know any better way to be Christian than to pray "in Jesus's name" in your devotions and with your words and through your life.

There was nothing conventional about Charlie Milford, at least not by the time we came to know him. His views would have been considered radical by many, but Charlie never hesitated to share. He was neither modest nor apologetic about what he believed. Not long after we met Charlie, he informed us that he was resurrecting the Humility Club, and we were invited. For three or four years, the last years of the Humility Club's existence, I attended faithfully, and I earned some stock along the way by holding my own in sparring with the veterans. To say the conversations were non-traditional for Baptist ministers would be an understatement, and I learned early to take things in stride (not knowing how often the views shared were a test for the novice, to see how much they could make me wince or flinch!). But when Charlie said, "Everything that's true about Christianity is a myth," I have to admit it caught me off guard.

Well, if you've been with me from the beginning of this book, you know by now that I've been on the journey quite a while, that I'm miles from where I started—but it took me a while to let this one sink in. Maybe (because he knew it rubbed me a little wrong) that's why he kept saying it in front of me! But the more we talked about what Charlie meant about "truth" and "Christianity" and "myth," and from hearing the stories of his life and coming to understand his convictions of faith, by how he had lived, I grew to embrace even this bold "heresy." (A heresy is just an affirmation that runs counter to orthodoxy, which is just the prevailing view [a majority opinion] for any day—which means orthodoxies are not necessarily right, and heresies are not necessarily wrong!)

In wrangling with Charlie, I came to understand that truth is deeper than words. Dietrich Bonhoeffer spoke of the God who is beyond "God," which is to say that the only way to form concepts and images of God is by the use of our words, but regardless of the integrity of those words, no matter how close they might come, theoretically, to truly describing God (and how close could the finite words of finite creatures come to describing the infinite?), no words about "God" are actually God.

In a sermon titled "Just Because It Didn't Happen Doesn't Mean It Isn't True," Rev. Beth Ellen Cooper tells the following story from Buddhist lore:

> The nun Wu Jincang asked the Sixth Patriarch Huineng, "I have studied the Mahaparinirvana sutra for many years, yet there are many areas I do not quite understand. Please enlighten me."
>
> The patriarch responded, "I am illiterate. Please read out the characters to me, and perhaps I will be able to explain the meaning."
>
> Said the nun, "You cannot even recognize the characters. How are you able then to understand the meaning?"
>
> The Patriarch replied: "Truth has nothing to do with words. Truth can be likened to the bright moon in the sky. Words, in this case, can be likened to a finger. The finger can point to the moon's location. However, the finger is not the moon. To look at the moon, it is necessary to gaze beyond the finger, right?"[2]

So if words are not God and if they can, ultimately, only *point* to truth, how should we understand the words of faith? Thomas Moore is not afraid to use the word "myth": "A myth is a sacred story…describing in fictional form the fundamental truths of nature and human life. Mythology gives body to the invisible and eternal factors that are always part of life but don't appear in a literal, factual story."[3] And I love the definition I have heard attributed to Frederick Buechner: A myth is a Truth that can never be proven, but can only be lived for, believed in and loved.

Myth may not suit you as a reference to faith, but I would challenge you to reconsider. How else would you characterize, categorize the words of faith? Consider…

Nothing that is true about Christianity can be proven—neither God nor the divinity of Jesus nor the presence of Spirit, not the miracles or salvation or sin or grace or forgiveness. Everything that is true about Christianity, then, must be something other than "fact"—and would we want it to be otherwise? If God *could* be *proven*, wouldn't that change the nature of what God is? Only temporal, material events or processes can be tested empirically and proven factually (the theory of gravity, the process of evolution). Mathematically, theorems can be proven; equations can be solved. But is that how we want to understand God—as some temporal, testable, provable part of the material universe, some kind of abstract equation, an intellectual theory?

The poet Wallace Stevens once said, "The final belief is to believe in a fiction, which you know to be a fiction, there being nothing else. The exquisite truth is to know that it is a fiction and that you believe in it willingly."[4] I understand that this quotation—and the implication that any matter of faith, maybe especially God, is a "fiction"—will be offensive to some people, but do we really want to try to place matters of faith in the category of "fact"?

I do not.

The definition of faith according to that great "faith chapter" in Hebrews 11 speaks to this point: *Now faith is the assurance of things* hoped *for, the conviction of things not seen.* If you can prove a thing, there is no need for hope (in fact, there can be no hope)—and where would human beings be without hope? Psychologists and others in the medical profession know that hope is essential to survival. This was proven for survivors of the Holocaust—when a prisoner lost all hope, death was almost guaranteed.

Furthermore, almost nothing that really matters in this world is "seeable" (physical, tangible, material, hence "provable")—love, truth, hope, trust, justice, grace, relationships, God. Those characteristics and experiences and moments that make life meaningful and purposeful are inevitably "spiritual" in nature, not material. Even an ardent atheist should agree with this.

The North Carolina singer/songwriter David Wilcox addresses this truth about faith in a beautiful old song called "Hold It Up to the Light." In this lyric, Wilcox reflects on a moment of decision, a "crossroad" that has him stumped. As he struggles in indecision, he turns to God, and the singer understands what many of the faithful do not about what really constitutes faith:

I said, "God, will you bless this decision?
I'm scared, is my life at stake?
But I see if you gave me a vision
I would never have reason to use my faith."
…so I'll hold it up to the light.[5]

I do not want a God who is *provable*. Whatever it might be, anything that is literally provable could not be God as I understand the divine. I do not want a faith that really is just a fact that some people can't see. As I have come to understand it, in part thanks to Charlie Milford's unorthodox belief, "faith" and "fact" must be, in essence, different things.

That being true, though it took me a while not to flinch at his words too, I'll go with Wallace Stevens, that "the final [the most important, the ultimate] belief [and doesn't belief imply faith?] is to believe [to completely cast your hope[in a fiction [because faith cannot be proven]."

How have the greatest truths that humans have tried to communicate always been conveyed? In stories—fiction! There are the ancient myths of Greece and Rome, which are taught in every high school in America not because they comport with the religion of most Americans, but because these stories convey great truths of human longing and achievement, joy and struggle, life and death. Those truths are also conveyed in the great legends of every culture, in Aesop's fables, in the Brothers Grimm folktales, even in Mother Goose nursery rhymes. And in our own day, what about *The Chronicles of Narnia* and the wild popularity of the *Harry Potter* series and *The Hunger Games*, not to mention every paperback love story, every motion picture drama? And what about those great stories told by Tim McGraw in his song, *Live Like You Were Dying*? A man speaks of a diagnosis that means the end of his life may be sooner than imagined, so he got busy living: skydiving, mountain climbing, bullriding...

> And I loved deeper, and I spoke sweeter, and I gave forgiveness I'd been denying."
> And he said, "Someday I hope you get the chance to live like you were dying."[6]

Except for Narnia, none of the stories I've just mentioned is Christian in nature, but the point is that they all convey deep, universal human truths. The American novelist Tom Robbins understood the power of fiction, the essence of story, when he said, "Just because it didn't happen doesn't mean that it isn't true."[7]

What about the sower and the seed, the prodigal son? The fact that there wasn't a literal farmer, a literal father has no bearing on the truth found in these parables. What about the creation narratives of Genesis? That they don't completely correspond to the current understandings of cosmology says absolutely nothing of their ability to convey ultimate truth. What about the resurrection? (Stay with me, please!) Even for the most hard-core literalist, there is more to the Easter story than the "fact" of resurrection. In other words, even for those who take this story as incontrovertible, historical fact, the greatest miracle in the history of the world, there is more to the story than "just the facts, ma'am."[8] Even for the most fervent literalist, "rising from the dead" can be used as a metaphor referring to the power of God in our lives. You might hear a rhetorical question like "When has God raised *you* 'from the dead'?" in the most conservative churches in America. Even fundamentalist pastors might ask, "When has Jesus 'spoken to you' and, like Mary on that Easter morning, you didn't recognize him?"

To speak of myth is not necessarily to discount a story's historical factuality; it is to say that the purpose of the story is to convey more than just the *facts* of the story. I believe every story in Scripture, from Genesis to Revelation, is about more than the facts. By that I simply mean the facts are not what is most important—there is a message, the truth of which supersedes the importance of any facts.

Some of the stories of the Bible may be less than fact as well. Of course there are the parables of the New Testament, the legends of the Old Testament, and nearly all biblical scholars now agree that the genre "Gospel" means those four narratives about the life of Jesus—attributed to Matthew, Mark, Luke, and John—are not biographies of his life, but theological interpretations. For several centuries anxious scholars played gymnastics with the texts, "harmonizing" the Gospels to explain away the discrepancies, the birth narratives that do not agree, wildly differing chronologies of events, the same stories told with conflicting essential details, resurrection narratives that even reveal doubt among the eyewitnesses, etc.

These conflicts are only a problem today for the most uninformed literalists—because if the purpose of the gospel is theology and not bibliography, it simply doesn't matter. The writers were not concerned about chronology and history and geography and biology. Their concern was far more important. Their concern was faith in Jesus!

Mark's Jesus seems the most human, though even this, the oldest Gospel, begins by identifying Jesus as *the son of God* (Mark 1). Matthew is trying to convince his mostly Jewish audience that Jesus is the long-awaited Jewish Messiah. Luke is speaking to a Gentile crowd about a savior for the poor and the outcast. John's theological, highly symbolic Gospel, written several decades after the others, benefits from Christological development in those years and the growth of a nascent Christian community. As most scholars now understand it, there are no conflicting facts in these divergent Gospels—because adherence to facts was never important to begin with.

Everything that is true about Christianity is a myth—because the stories of our Scripture, the convictions of our faith, the movements of Spirit have never been about fact. On the one side are those who say God is provable because there *are* facts, and if only we believe, we will see them. On the other side are those who dare to "*walk by faith, not by sight*" (2 Cor 5:7), courageously giving themselves to a "fiction that you believe in willingly," because "Truth… can never be proven…only…lived for, believed in and loved." I'll take the latter position any day, faith-as-fiction, because calling it *myth* is the best way I know how to be honest about what faith really means.

Trinity—Math or Myth?

Why I Still Believe

Isaiah 6:1–8; Romans 8:12–17

Russ Dean, May 25, 2003

Math—"the study of the measurement, properties, and relationships of quantities, using numbers and symbols."[9] Math is the language of all that is *empirical*—that which can be seen, known, measured, evaluated, defined. 2 + 2 = 4. Math always "adds up."[10]

Math is *essential* in our world. (I am glad some people actually understand it!) The economies of all the world's cultures are dependent upon math: 2 + 2 = life (or death). And the advancing understanding of math led the scientific revolution that gave birth to a world of "enlightenment." The theories of Copernicus, his "math problems," born out by observation and testing, led to the reframing of our entire universe. *We* are not the center of it all.

We moderns were born in the light of mathematics, out of the Dark Ages of superstition, fear, and magic. And math, this world's great intellectual midwife, continues her work, as scientists, whose titles I can hardly pronounce, write equations, whose terms I cannot even read, in pursuit of formulas, whose answers, like that of Copernicus, will continue to give birth to vast new worlds of understanding and life. Some wildly optimistic mathematicians, in fact, hold out hope that at the heart of the universe there is one formula (maybe one *simple* formula) that defines the very meaning of life.[11]

Math is the language of all that is *empirical*—that which can be seen, known, measured, evaluated, defined. Math always "adds up."

Myth—the word is grossly misunderstood and scarcely used in the modern church. It conveys to many people the idea of that which is make-believe, a statement or story or proposition which is in opposition to fact. Such a definition could hardly be more incorrect. The word *myth* is one that the church ought to reclaim with passion and excitement. The word *myth* is one that the Church *must* learn if we are to relearn the art of reading the Bible in a highly mathematical world. Let me share with you several definitions.

From Thomas Moore:

A myth is a sacred story…describing in fictional form the fundamental truths of nature and human life. Mythology gives body to the invisible and eternal factors that are always part of life but don't appear in a literal, factual story.[12]

From Joseph Campbell:

People say that what we're all seeking is a meaning for life…. I think that what we're seeking is an experience of being alive, so that our life experiences on the purely physical plane will have resonances within our own innermost being and reality, so that we actually feel the rapture of being alive. That's what it's all finally about, and…myths are clues to the spiritual potentialities of the human life.[13]

In the old police drama *Dragnet*, Joe Friday was famous for saying, "Just the facts, ma'am. Just the facts."[14] But *Truth* can never be contained in "just the facts." So it is, then, that only through "myth" do finite minds approach The Eternal. As a language in itself *myth* lacks the definitive, fact-*only*, empirical value of the grammar of mathematics. I love Frederick Buechner's definition: A myth is "a Truth that can never be proven" (which is the very point of math—to prove equations)—myth is a truth that "can only be lived for, believed in and loved."[15]

If matters of faith could, in fact, be *proven*, we could simply gather on Sundays and recite mathematical formulas to one another. There would be no need for worship in that setting; we would just convene to "solve for"[16] a god who did not need to be believed in. To "solve for" a god who did not call to be lived for. To "solve for" a god who could not beckon us to love.

Give me the beauty and the potential of *myth*—any day—and I will gladly accept the tension and ambiguity, the great risk of misunderstanding that will *always* be inherent to such language.

Myth is the language of faith.

In a conversation that extends back to our first eight-hour interview with the search committee here, I have consistently defined myself, over against a unitarian position (a theology defined by the radical Oneness of God), as a *Trinitarian* Christian. Trinity: "The union of three divine persons, the Father, Son, and Holy Spirit, in one God."[17] Three. In. One.

Trinity—math or myth?

A study of the history of the Trinitarian debate makes the definition of this three-in-one proposition even more confusing. It's almost comical! (Bear with me for one brief trivial pursuit.) The heated debate raged through the fourth and fifth centuries over the definitions of the Greek and Latin terms for *substance, essence,* and *person.* At the heart of the controversy were two bishops. Arius claimed that Christ was of a similar substance to God. He used the Greek word *homoiousios.* Athanasius, on the other hand (whose argument eventually prevailed), believed Christ was of the very same substance as God— *homoousios.* All of the fighting was over two words, spelled identically, except for one letter, the Greek "iota." You've heard the expression "an iota's difference"—it comes from this theological debate.

St. Augustine once remarked, "All these theories sought to speak of things that cannot be uttered, and [because of all the confusion] the Trinity is a favorite target of critics out to show the logical incoherence of Christianity."[18] For example, a Muslim cleric addressed American troops in the Persian Gulf War, "Your clergy tell you that Christian belief is founded on the doctrine of the Trinity, but when you ask them to explain it, they tell you it is a mystery. If they cannot explain it, then why should you continue to believe in such nonsense?"[19]

Neither is critique of the doctrine limited to non-Christian skeptics. Bishop John Shelby Spong voices this word of caution: "I…support efforts to reexamine and perhaps even to transcend the Trinitarian compromise, if those now-literalized words prove to be no longer capable of leading us into the experience of God toward which they originally pointed."[20]

I am not yet ready to "transcend the Trinitarian compromise," but I do believe the controversial bishop is correct when he asserts that the words of Trinitarian language, as with much else representing Christian orthodoxy, have today become so literalized that they very often fail to point Christians to "the *experience* of God."

Trinity—math or myth?

Where did this language of Trinity come from? Why has it been deemed essential to Christian thought for seventeen centuries? Why is it still relevant today?

Very early after the death of Jesus, his followers began to testify to an experience of God—not to some abstract notion of God—an experience that they had not known before Jesus. God was "Creator," far and removed. Transcendent and powerful. Untouchable. Fearful. But in Jesus they saw the face of God. In Jesus they heard how God talked. They saw where God walked. They witnessed how God loves. In Jesus they found Immanuel—God with us.

And after Jesus had left them gathered together in Jerusalem, this ragged but now radically empowered band of misfit followers experienced, *again*, the presence of God. This time, not in the awe of a Creator, not in the flesh of a Redeemer, but in the moving, unexplainable-yet-undeniable presence of a sustaining Spirit—*within* them.

This three-fold experience of God—an experience that the early church insisted could not be adequately conveyed in speaking only of "One God"—led to the defining of a doctrine called *Trinity*.

I believe this three-fold experience of God is still revelatory, still relevant, still reliable today. But the language of a "Triune God" is not mathematics. It never has been.[21] The language of Trinity is mythological—that is, it points beyond itself to a God who can never be fully defined.[22] Who can never be delimited by tidy formulas. Who will never be proven mathematically. The three-in-one God is a God who can only be proven in the living—"believed in, lived for, and loved."

Trinity—math or myth?

The language of Trinity developed out of a people's experience of God—a living and dynamic experience that is still accessible. But in this debate, another vitally important insight was achieved. In his book *When Religion Becomes Evil*, Charles Kimball says of the radical monotheism of Islam: "The most heinous sin in Islam is *shirk* ('associating something with God'). God is one.... There is no God but God."[23] Much as their Jewish brothers and sisters do, Islam insists on a radical unitarianism—God alone is God. And so…

"God is alone."[24]

It was precisely this kind of *alone* (and, therefore, lonely), *absolute* (and, therefore, unsympathetic) Divine *Power* that Athanasius rejected. He insisted that we could not speak of the God who was revealed in Jesus Christ, and who is continually experienced through the Holy Spirit, as this kind of Lonely, Absolute, Autocratic Dictator on High. Trinitarian theology rejected a God who is distant and isolated, unsharing and unshared, static and unchanging. In a Trinitarian God the church discovered *community*, for they discovered a radically different God, who models, within God's very nature, equality, sharing, mutual accountability, risk, vulnerability, need.[25] Yes, need. Far from the static, absolute God of Power who needs nothing, the Trinitarian God needs *community*.[26] In the Trinitarian God, community is the highest Truth; community is the greatest good.

If you are still unconvinced, I ask you to consider what is lost in our Christian theology if we do *not* use the word "Trinity" to speak of God? And let me give you my three-fold answer: 1) I believe we lose our greatest argument for the importance of sharing and equality and mutual respect—for the Trinitarian God *is* community. 2) I believe we lose our greatest argument for an *inclusive* God—a God who not only tolerates but invites diversity and pluralism of thought—for the three-in-one God is unity—but *unity in diversity*. 3) I believe we lose our greatest argument that God is love, and that this Love, therefore, calls us to make God real for a world who cannot believe—for the Triune God *is* sacrifice and risk and vulnerability and need.

Trinity—math or myth?

Someone once said that it is not so much that God is "three in one" as opposed to "five in one" or "fifteen in one" but that God is not *just* one,[27] which is to say that God is never alone. The Christian experience of the Trinitarian God reveals a God who is "above us, with us, within us"[28]—and that experience of *community* and *diversity* and *love*—calls us beyond ourselves to a formula that never quite adds up in mathematical terms: *The two shall become one flesh* (Gen 2:24). *The first will be the last* (Mark 10:31). *The greatest will be the least* (Matt 23:11).

God—three in one.

Trinity—math or myth?

Myth. Always myth. So let us "believe it, live it, love it," even today.

May it be so.

PASTORAL PRAYER:
Speak to us, Great Triune God
   in your diversity—
         the God from beyond who Creates,
         the God among us who Redeems,
         the God within us who Sustains.
Speak to us, Great Triune God
   in your unity—
         the God of a Truth that is always a becoming,[28]

And in our communities,
   and in our very own hearts,
         call us to celebrate our diversity
         and to recognize our unity

That the world might know Your Peace.

Amen. Amen. Amen.

Notes

[1] Wallace Stevens, *Opus Posthumous: Poems, Plays, Prose* (New York: Random House, 2011), 189.

[2] Rev. Beth Ellen Cooper, "Just Because It Didn't Happen Doesn't Mean It Isn't True," *Keep the Faith* (blog), *Houston Chronicle*, December 14, 2011, http://blog.chron.com/keepthefaith/2011/12/just-because-it-didnt-happen-doesnt-mean-it-isnt-true/.

[3] Moore, Thomas, *Care of the Soul—A Guide For Cultivating Depth and Sacredness in Everyday Life* (New York: HarperCollins, 1992), 220.

[4] Stevens, Wallace, *Opus Posthumous: Poems, Plays, Prose* (New York: Random House, 2011), 189.

[5] David Wilcox. "Hold It Up to the Light," *Big Horizon*. A&M Records, 1994.

[6] Tim McGraw, "Live Like You Were Dying," *Live Like You Were Dying*. Curb Records, 2004.

[7] Vigorito, Tony, "The Syntax of Sorcery: An Interview with Tom Robbins," *Reality Sandwich Is Psychedelic Culture*, June 6, 2012, (https://realitysandwich.com/150587/syntax_sorcery_interview_tom_robbins/.

[8] These words are attributed to the fictitious Sergeant Joe Friday on the old detective drama, *Dragnet*, though apparently the words were never uttered in an episode but made famous in a 1953 radio parody called "St. George and the Dragonet" by Stan Freberg.

[9] Author, "Math," *The American Heritage College Dictionary*, (Boston, MA: Houghton Mifflin, 1993).

[10] A mathematician in our congregation has already taken issue with my definition of math as "always adding up." The theories of advanced mathematics, calculus, physics, etc., certainly open a world that is less than "definitive," yet I stand by my usage of math as such—for the sake of my argument that the Trinity is not simply about the numbers (3 in 1).

[11] As little as I understand of the advancing formulas of the quantum sciences, I know that there are some scientists/mathematicians who believe that the universe will one day be explained by one great unifying theory that can be represented by a mathematical formula (in the same way that E=MC2 is a "definitive" formula).

[12] Thomas Moore, *Care Of The Soul—A Guide For Cultivating Depth And Sacredness In Everyday Life* (New York: HarperCollins, 1995), 220.

[13] Joseph Campbell with Bill Moyers, *The Power of Myth* (New York: Anchor Books Doubleday, 1988), 5.

[14] See footnote 8.

[15] This definition connects us to our recent conversations on "belief." Is believing (in resurrection, or God, or Trinity) just a matter of mental assent, or is there an experiential quality that is required? This positive understanding of myth has led one interpreter to conclude, "Everything that is true about Christianity is a myth" (Charlie Milford), which is not to *deny* anything, but to push Christian faith into the realm of the "more than." More than fact. More than history. More than mental understanding.

[16] In algebra, students learn to "solve for X," an unknown quantity that can be determined by proper manipulation of the numbers and terms of the equation.

[17] Author, "Trinity," *The American Heritage College Dictionary*, (Boston, MA: Houghton Mifflin, 1993).

[18] William C. Placher, *A History of Christian Thought: An Introduction* (Louisville, KY: Westminster John Knox Press, 1983), 79.

[19] Quoted in J. Robert Wright, "Why Believe Still in The Trinity?," *The Living Pulpit*, Vol. 8 No.2 (April–June 1999), 38.

[20] John Shelby Spong, *Why Christianity Must Change or Die: A Bishop Speaks to Believers In Exile* (San Francisco: HarperOne, 1999), 19.

[21] I have argued in a number of recent conversations that the *language* of Christian faith has *always* been "mythological" in character. Even the language of the creeds, the very early language that gave shape to Christian theology, has always had a more-than-literal character. It might be tempting to believe than in our "advanced" and modern world, we have a better grasp of faith than did our poor, prescientific forebears, who thought only in literal, concrete terms. I think this is a huge mistake in understanding. In the bulletin of today's worship service, I used the following quotation as justification for this point: "[Speaking of the Holy Trinity] When it is asked three what, then the great poverty from which our language suffers becomes apparent. But the formula three persons was coined not in order to give a complete explanation by means of it, but in order that we might not be obliged to remain silent" (Gregory Nazianzus, 325–389 C.E.). Even in the fourth century Trinitarian language was not about mathematics!

[22] I thought here of our conversation on the Ten Commandments and the prohibition against creating "graven images." In that discussion we talked of language and theological images as potential "graven images"—images that sought to be too definitive of God and could, therefore, become idolatrous in themselves.

[23] Charles Kimball, *When Religion Becomes Evil: Five Warning Signs* (San Francisco and New York: HarperOne, 2008), 43.

[24] Ibid.

[25] The critic will certainly ask if we ever really discover God or if we simply continue to "create God in *our image*." I am aware of this tension yet believe that God's nature is, to some extent, *revealed* in human experience. I also admit, however, that theological language and structures are *created*. We live in faith, dependent upon, and influenced by, the frameworks for our understandings of and relationships to God, developed in this tension between the *revealed* and the *created*. Therefore, I stand by the Trinitarian formulation, confusing as it may be, as crucially important to an inclusive, fully Christian understanding of God.

[26] For this insight, and much of my understanding of the Trinitarian debate, I am indebted to Arthur C. McGill in his book, *Suffering: A Test of Theological Method*, chapter titled, "Athanasius and Arias: A Study in Contrasts," (Philadelphia: Westminster Press, 1982), 80-82.

[27] Dr. Bob Ratcliffe of Candler School of Theology at Emory University.

[28] Wright, *The Living Pulpit*, 39.

[29] "Truth is more a becoming than it is a having" has become an important statement for this church's understanding of theology and its pursuit of knowing God.

A New Faith: Leaving the Blood In

Questions to Consider

When you were a child, did you learn that Jesus died on the cross? Do you remember how you felt about this (frightened, angry, sad, confused)?

When did you begin to learn a theology (i.e., what Jesus's death meant) about Jesus's death? Do you remember how you felt about that?

If you learned that "Jesus died for you," where was God in that picture?

Are there any of the teachings of the church that offend you? If so, what do you do with them? Would there be any way to rework or reform or redeem that theology?

What hymns or religious songs can you sing from memory? What theology do they teach you?

Do you ever sing anything in church with which you disagree?

What is the greatest gift anyone has ever given you?

Has anyone ever made a true sacrifice for you? Have you ever truly sacrificed for someone else?

What is the surest, deepest expression of love you have ever known?

❖

There is an atonement...in the [very] heart of God...
and out of this comes the forgiveness of our sins.
—Donald Baillie[1]

I was raised on "blood hymns." You may be able to sing along (you may not want to!):

"What can wash away my sins?
Nothing but the blood of Jesus!"[2]

***

"There is a fountain filled with blood, drawn from Immanuel's veins.
And sinners plunged beneath the flood lose all their guilty stains."[3]

***

"There is power, power, wonder-working power
in the blood (in the blood) of the Lamb (of the Lamb).
There is power, power, wonder-working power
in the precious blood of the Lamb.[4]

***

"The blood that gives me strength from day to day
will never lose its power."[5]

I just spit all of those lines out by memory, and if you were raised in a Baptist church like I was, you probably don't need a hymnal either. Since I'm no longer in a church that employs such a theology, however, it's been a while since I even thought about some of these lines, and I have to say that in just hearing them again, I can understand why some people would be offended—an entire fountain *filled* with…blood? Wow. That's graphic, if not downright grotesque.

Years ago I preached a sermon in which I shared my experience of witnessing an open-heart surgery. That surgery was a fascinating experience, and I had a front-row view standing at the patient's head, side by side with the nurse anesthetist. The cardiothoracic surgeon who was in my church had invited me. I didn't hesitate to get my free ticket for the show, which later seemed an appropriate illustration for a sermon about Israel's fierce, if fallen, King David, who was called *a man after God's own heart* (1 Sam 13:14; Acts 13:22).

"What is a good heart?," I asked in the sermon, which had about as little blood in it as the surgery I had witnessed. That day in the OR I had seen only about a teaspoon (okay, maybe a tablespoon!) in a procedure that included opening a forty-year-old woman's chest and suturing three veins around the blockages of her two-packs-a-day heart.

The surgery was amazing, the sermon illustration spot on, but after worship a woman in our choir told me she had almost gotten up to leave the loft, mid-sermon, feeling a bit queasy. "I don't do blood," she said—and she's not the only one. By theological tradition and musical history Park Road Baptist Church doesn't "do blood" either. I'm grateful.

I was raised on it, and I survived, but looking back I know I would have been better off without it. Maybe I could have even loved God without being afraid and followed Jesus without bearing years of emotional guilt for putting him up there on that cross: "Just as I am, without one plea but that thy blood *was shed for me.*"

For the first twenty-plus years of my life, I would not have understood the words I have just written. Jesus died for me. The Bible says it. Centuries of classical artwork reinforce it. The hymns that are the source of much of our internalized theology etch his bloody death and our shame and guilt onto our souls. Yes, it's grotesque. That's what the Romans intended. They carefully devised crucifixion to be an instrument of excruciating torture and over thousands of gruesome executions fine-tuned their sadistic tool to deepen and widen the evil of it. The depth of his pain only proved the power of his love. God planned it that way. So I was told.

Nor in my earlier years would I have understood the offense taken by a woman who thanked me for the "fine sermon" I had just delivered in her Unitarian Universalist church. She seemed almost surprised by my pulpiteering and by a sermon she could actually tolerate from a Baptist, but she found it hard to restrain her prejudice: "We have nothing against you," she said, smiling with polite, Southern condescension. "We just don't believe in divine child sacrifice." Such smug derision would have offended me for many of my early years, and that critique would have seemed as absurd as it was pagan. "*For God so love the world that he gave his only son*" (John 3:16).

Compounding the problem for some critics of Christianity are the words concerning communion: "*Very truly, I tell you, unless you eat the flesh of the Son of Man and drink his blood, you have no life in you*" (John 6:53). If you can escape the familiarity of the theology, prescribed by a lifetime of Lord's Supper ceremonies in church, you might understand why some people can only hear in Jesus's words a call to superstition or the voodoo of an ancient tribal cannibalism. We can be holier-than-thou about our religious tradition, but eating someone's flesh and drinking their blood is a pretty textbook definition of cannibalism. If Christians want to present our faith as accessible and meaningful in the modern world, we need to be ready to hear and understand the twenty-first-century critiques that will come.

The atonement theology/imagery that was at the heart of my early church experience is an offense to many people outside the church—and to many within the Christian tradition as well. There has been a growing conversation, even within evangelicalism, of the need to reframe the understanding of Jesus's death, placing less emphasis on "substitutionary atonement" (he died as a substitute for me) and more thought to some variation of what might be called "participatory atonement." For any who need some help understanding some of the criticism of substitutionary atonement, let me share a portion of one of my sermons from 2012, titled, "He Didn't Die for Nothing."

> I believe in God, the Father Almighty, creator of heaven and earth and in Jesus Christ, his only begotten son, our Lord, who was conceived by the Holy Spirit, born of the virgin Mary, suffered under Pontius Pilate, was crucified, died, and was buried; he descended into hell; on the third day he rose again from the dead...
>
> [These are the words of the Apostles' Creed, taken as a summation of orthodox doctrine by large portions of the church, but in this creed] where do we see the value of Jesus's life? His teaching? His healing? His example? His charismatic, grab-life-by-the-horns-and-hang-on-for-the-ride passion? Many see the Christianity of the creed as demeaning Jesus's life, reducing his living to have no real value. Such a view [that only his death matters] sends many cynics running as fast as they can. If his life was of no value, how can it speak to mine? That underestimation of his teaching and the example he lived, coupled with a bloody theology of Jesus's death, are a double-whammy that make Christian faith irredeemable for many in a twenty-first-century world.
>
> The critics say this theology makes God out to be a tyrant, demanding his pound of flesh for satisfaction, and makes of Christian salvation some kind of fear-filled blood sport. We ought to understand why those who did not grow up in Southern evangelical religion would wince, or maybe feel a bit sick to their stomachs, to hear Christians sing, "Are you washed in the blood, in the soul-cleansing blood of the Lamb?"

We who were raised "beneath the cross of Jesus" were given the justifications for our theology: "Because the Bible says." And though it is circular logic (it's true because the Bible says it, and the Bible says it because it's true), inside such a literalistic worldview, if the Bible says it, it's gospel truth.[6] Even respectable literalists, however, should be able to admit that the concerns and criticisms about the heart of that guilt-inducing revivalism ("Jesus shed his blood for me!") are valid. A God who demands someone's actual life in exchange for salvation is open to an understandable critique of being a blood-thirsty tyrant, not a loving father. On the backdrop of the child-sacrifice often practiced in the ancient world, and with the obvious allusions to the Abraham/

Isaac story as well as the cultic practice of first-century Judaism, animal slaughter as expiation for sins, my Unitarian friend's understandable, if haughty, response is also legitimate.

For thoughtful Christians, not just the critics of the religion, the arguments against such an understanding of atonement mount.

- If God created the world out of nothing and designed the rules by which we must live, why must atonement by death be the only way? And wouldn't God actually be responsible for the need for atonement to begin with, as well as for those who, as a result of the system, ultimately fail to be justified?

- Christians speak of salvation by grace, which is often defined as "unmerited favor," and in Christian history, long battles have been waged: "salvation by grace through faith" versus salvation by "works righteousness." Those who most ardently uphold the view of substitutionary atonement explicitly reject "works righteousness"—but if "*the wages of sin is death*" (Rom 6:23) and Jesus paid those wages with his life, could that salvation truly be "grace" (*unmerited* favor)? It might have been the "*free gift of God*" (Rom 6:23) for me—but it certainly wasn't free to Jesus! And if *anything* is required of anyone, it cannot honestly be called "free."

- The "love chapter" in 1 Corinthians 13 tells us that love *keeps no record of wrongs* (v. 5). If God is love (1 John 4:8), wouldn't it also be truth that "God keeps no record of wrongs"? So why is any atonement needed at all? Wouldn't unconditional love have to be truly *without condition*?

- Finally, in a dense and powerful article, Mark Heim shows through a careful analysis that Jesus's teachings echoed the prophetic Jewish tradition, which had for centuries offered a critique of the Jewish cultic system of blood sacrifice: "*To obey is better than sacrifice*" (1 Sam 15:22). *With what shall I come before the LORD?... Shall I give my firstborn for my transgression?... God has told you what is good...do justice, love mercy, walk humbly with God* (Mic 6:6–8). In line with the prophetic tradition, it was Jesus's intention to overturn and subvert the sacrificial system, so Heim argues that if Jesus's death just becomes the final, perfect sacrifice, rather than overthrowing the system, his death becomes the ultimate validation of it. As the ultimate victim, Jesus's death justifies, even glorifies, the very system of redemptive violence that was his life's mission to destroy. Heim says, "The gospel...is not ultimately about the exchange of victims [Christ in our place], but about ending the bloodshed."[7]

Continuing with my 2012 sermon…

I understand those concerns. I share those concerns. But the Swiss theologian Emil Brunner says of the doctrine of the atonement that it is "the Christian religion itself; it is the main point; it is not something alongside of the center; it is the substance and the kernel, not the husk."[8] While sophisticated twenty-first-century critical-thinking Christians may look with contempt on such an opinion, this is just fact. From the beginning, Jesus's death has been the lynch pin of the faith called by his name. As powerful as it was, it was *not* Jesus's life that created a movement, so much as it was his death and its surprising aftermath.

The followers of the *living* Jesus were Jews. Paul was the earliest disciple, whose training in critical thinking as a Pharisee caused him to begin wrestling with Jesus's death—asking if it actually had any *meaning*—and in a stunning, offensive, heretical break with his Jewish teaching, he soon pronounced that Jesus's death was not a curse as the Law claimed in the book of Deuteronomy (21:23), but the death of Jesus was, itself, the very path to life.

Christianity—even in its very best form—is inseparable from the death of Jesus. And Jesus's horrifying death, properly understood, was not in vain, was not for nothing, because it opens to us a breathtaking view into the heart of God. This is a view that is *not* accessible, a view that could not be known in looking only at Jesus's *life*....

Liberal Christians often denounce the death of Jesus in such a way as to preclude that revelation. Maybe this is a case of throwing the baby out with the (bloody) bathwater! And as I've said to you, I understand that reflex, but I want to invite you, especially you who want to roll your eyes at such theology, who feel like slamming your hymnal shut every time you see the word "blood," who want to put your fingers in your ears when you hear the preacher even hint at atonement...I want to invite you to listen again.

Donald Baillie says, "There is an atonement, an expiation, in the [very] heart of God...and out of this comes the forgiveness of our sins."[9]

His statement needs careful thought before you scoff and discard it. The Christian God is not a demanding, blood-thirsty tyrant. Jesus did not save us from God by dying on a Roman cross for our sins. God did not send Jesus to the earth for the express purpose of dying.[10] And the Christian God is not a distant, foreboding, fearful, all-powerful deity who throws his power around manipulating things and events at his divine whim.[11] Quite the contrary.

Scripture makes the simple but audacious claim that *God is love* (1 John 4:7), and any love that will not expose itself to the vulnerability of suffering...any love that is not ultimately self-giving...any love that would simply refuse *to lay down its life for its friends* (John 15:13) is not really love. As you surely have known by your lived experience, true love is always hard...it is always costly...sometimes it is even bloody. Regardless your Christology, if Jesus represents God for us—then Jesus's death becomes the clearest prism into the heart of the Divine.

God is...self-sacrificial love.

We were sitting in the hall of a hotel in Dayton, Ohio. There was a Baptist meeting going on. I'm not sure if the sessions were over or if we were "cutting class," but the theological dialogue with my friend Dr. John Ballenger never ends. We were talking about bad hymnody (I know, preachers know how to party!). As we took particular umbrage at the "blood hymns," John's insight pierced the air. I will never forget his words.

Several of John's pithy wisdoms stay with me. I had seen a movie with a horrific plot involving racially inspired murder, and I said, "Tell me this doesn't really happen." John, who understands life and literature and the gritty relationship between the two, soberly replied, "It's hard to write stories about things that haven't happened in real life." Let that sink in. In another story that ended tragically he reminded me, "All true stories end in death." Ouch. In the hallway of a Dayton hotel, John changed my life again: "If it were up to me, I'd take all the blood hymns out. But I'd have to find a way to leave the blood in."

We can complain about the blood hymns. I think we should. We can critique the theology of substitutionary atonement. There is a better way to understand the death of Jesus. We can be sensitive to the abuse and misuse of theology. Even as a critic of the blood hymns, however, I have become convinced that there is a powerful lesson bound to the center of that theology, a truth we risk losing if we simply abandon it all at the accusation of bad theology.

It was Thanksgiving Day 1996, and I had just sprinted down the long hallway to the hospital waiting room: "It's a boy…9 pounds, 5 ounces…we had a boy!" After the customary congratulations, I sprinted back to labor and delivery to get my hands on our little Thanksgiving turkey, and when I walked into the room…oh my. Maybe I was in the wrong room, I thought. Maybe I accidently turned in to the operating room or the emergency room. You see, there was blood. And it was everywhere. I'm sorry to say this. (Maybe you'll have to run out of the choir loft!) But the floor was covered. Blood was on the table with all the doctor's tools. It was on the bed.

I learned later that a nurse had accidentally turned over a pan—but this only means that I got to see what usually, carefully and antiseptically, gets hidden from fathers. That room was painted in my wife's blood. It was a mother's blood that taught me in that moment what I had only heard as a truism before, that birth, there can be no doubt, is a labor of love. And love is… bloody.

"I'd have to find a way to leave the blood in."

Exactly.

For without the shedding of blood there is no remission of sins (Heb 9:22), because love that is not costly is not love. True love is always sacrificial—so Jesus's life, a commitment that only comes into clear focus through his death, did not save us from God's wrath. But like the firefighter who dies in the act of saving the child from the burning building, it was a sacrifice[12] because it was neither required nor necessary. And if Jesus can teach us through his death that only "*those who lose their life will keep it*" (Luke 17:33), then he *did* die "for us"—in order to teach us the very nature and love of God.

The atonement in the heart of God is not the blood of Jesus; it is sacrificial love, whenever, wherever, by whomever it is given, "for it is in giving that we receive, it is in pardoning that we are pardoned, it is in dying that we are born to eternal life."[13]

*Finding a Way to Leave the
Blood In*

Exodus 12:21–27; Romans 5:1–11

Russ Dean, October 5, 2008

It may be that of all the titles of Jesus, the images that have survived and grown in the mind of the church, the image of Jesus as our savior is the most powerful. In the birth narrative of Jesus from the book of Matthew, we read that an angel comes to Joseph and warns him that his espoused wife, his fiancée, will *"bear a son."* The angel gives instruction: *"You are to name him Jesus, for he will save his people from their sins"* (Matt 1:21). The history of the name Jesus is fascinating. Some believe the name, which derives from Latin, was corrupted in the translation from its Hebrew source, the name Yeshua. This name, Yeshua, is related to the longer form, Yehoshua (Joshua). The Hebrew noun *shua* means "a saving cry" or "a cry for help," and the prefix Yeho derives from the divine name Yahweh, so Yehoshua can be translated, literally, "'God' is a saving cry."

Jesus—Yeshua—as the one who *saves* is perhaps the image and identity of Jesus that has been most proclaimed by the church. We hear it in powerful, eloquent sermons, in densely theological essays, and in the crudely simple claim, "Jesus saves"—which we find ubiquitously scrawled across our culture: spray-painted on bridges, overpasses; scratched on exposed rocks on mountain roadsides; printed on posterboards held in the end zone of professional football games. As a promotion worthy of bumper sticker theology, "Jesus Saves" is hard to beat.

This notion that Jesus saves us by knowingly, personally dying for us is one that has been mined as gold by evangelists the world over. Many of you, as I, have been told that while he was hanging there in agony, he was thinking of…me. And the power of that deeply individualistic, highly emotional appeal is undeniable. Thousands have made personal professions of faith in Jesus because of such an appeal.

But this notion has not gone without critique—even within the evangelical church, which has polished the claim to a perfect shine. In recent years a number of evangelical scholars have taken on the notion of a substitutionary atonement—the idea that in some kind of literal, concrete way, God sent Jesus for the express purpose of dying for you. The notion has a crude, barbaric quality—what parent would determine from the outset such an inhuman, unthinkable end for a child? What kind of tyrant does such a theology make of God? And how is the freedom, the individuality, of Jesus destroyed if he had no choice in this mission? In their book *Recovering the Scandal of the Cross*, Joel Green and Mark Baker say, "We believe that the popular fascination with and commitment to penal substitutionary Atonement (that is, that Jesus was punished by God, in our place) has had ill effects in the life of the church in the United States and has little to offer the local church and mission by way of understanding or embodying the message of Jesus Christ."[14]

That popular fascination perhaps reached its zenith, or its nadir (whichever your perspective), its evangelistic high or its vulgar low ebb, in Mel Gibson's movie of a few years ago, *The Passion of the Christ*, which has enough gratuitous violence, enough sadistic torture and needless suffering to satisfy even an American audience—engorged as we are in our ongoing orgy of violence. And there's enough blood in the movie to sink the proverbial battleship.

Very near the center of Christian theology is the notion of atonement—our "at-one-ment" with God, made possible by Jesus. This doctrine has been worked out over the centuries in a *number* of different atonement theories, each with scriptural justification—yet because the church in our part of the world has centered its focus on only one of these, we hardly even know that Christians have always thought, variously, about the death of Jesus. Intrinsically connected to all of these doctrines *is* the cross of Christ—but is the blood what it's really all about? Must we feast in the blood and gore of an emotionally laden substitution to understand God's work among us in Jesus? Writing for the mainline Protestant publication *The Christian Century*, writer and scholar Mark Heim agrees with a growing number of evangelical theologians who say no. Heim believes that the story of Jesus—which necessarily includes his life, his death, and his resurrection—the whole story of Jesus when taken together with the ancient wisdom of our sacred Scripture combine to tell us that Jesus's message is that the mechanism of scapegoating has no place in the life of a God of unconditional love, unmerited favor, unending forgiveness.[15]

In the book of John, the high priest Caiaphas says to his colleagues, *What are we to do* [with this Jesus]*?... You do not understand that it is better for you to have one man die for the people than to have the whole nation destroyed* (John 11:49). And so it is that a framework of scapegoating is built around the death of Jesus. Given the Jewish origin of Christian faith, with its ancient practice of blood sacrifice—a bloody image of such salvation, which reaches back at least as far as the story of the Passover (today's Old Testament text)—it is no surprise that Christian faith, in seeking to make sense of the death of Jesus, reached for such images to interpret his death. But as Mark Heim says, if Jesus just becomes the final, ultimate victim, a "bigger and better" victim in this ungodly machine, rather than tearing down the mechanism of scapegoating, we build it up. Rather than Jesus's death signaling the end of divine violence, the crucifixion becomes the highest justification of it.

In his well-acclaimed series *The Chronicles of Narnia*, the late C. S. Lewis tries to make this point. Aslan, the lion hero, is slain on the sacrificial altar—slain, supposedly, by his enemies, in place of his friends. Of course, his enemies have another idea altogether in mind. Rather than Aslan being a *substitute*, they intend for Aslan's friends to be next. Violence only begets violence in such a mechanism. There can be no end to the killing. But in the rising of Aslan, that sacrificial stone itself is torn to pieces. Resurrection signals the destruction of such a broken system—broken under the weight of innocent suffering. So it is that, in Jesus, the whole notion of scapegoating sacrifice—the one given for the many—is destroyed.

I am utterly convinced that until the church can disabuse itself of the notion of God-sanctioned violence—even violence which is *supposed* to end all violence—I am convinced that any God-sanctioned violence ultimately gives justification for all other violence. Because of the *life* of Jesus, the death of Jesus must tell us that God did not, does not, intend this. Yes, *God is at work in all things, to bring about good* (Rom 8:28)—but this was not God's idea. We need to rid ourselves of our violent theology, our gory belief, and, yes, our bloody hymns that support such violence.

But in a meaningful conversation a few years ago with a dear seminary friend, we were discussing this very idea—of ridding the church of such a bloody theology—when John made a profoundly helpful comment: "If it were up to me," he said, "I'd do away with all the 'blood hymns' [as they are some-times called], but I'd have to find a way to leave the blood in."

I'd have to find a way to leave the blood in!

You see, without blood there is no life. It is the stream which carries us from one breath to the next. It is the source of our strength. And though we must be careful how we speak of it, careful that our language does not end up justifying violence, blood is often inseparable from our salvation. Jesus said, *There is no greater love…than love which lays down its life…love which parts with its own blood—for the sake of a friend* (John 15:13). Perhaps we cannot truly understand life, know the meaning of real love, until we have experienced this…in blood. Someone else's blood, shed for us…or our blood, shed for another.

Twelve years ago an ecstatic, young, first-time father dashed to the waiting room to give the great news—*for unto us a child is born!* (Isa 9:6). Cheers went up all around—a son, 9 pounds, 5 ounces—hurray! Returning to the labor and delivery room (a room well-named!), the father was not prepared for what he would witness there. A room covered in blood. A nurse had accidentally overturned a pan, and it looked like a war scene. It was the blood of labor. The blood of life. Blood given freely. Blood which tells the story of…salvation.

Jackson Russell Dean is here because of it. And so are you and I.

The heart of atonement theology is this: Sometimes we can't go it alone. Despite the confidence of our birth, our creation in the *image of God* (Gen 1:27), the *new creation* we become in Christ (2 Cor 5:17)—despite all our individual strength, sometimes we need to be saved. Sometimes our parents do this for us. Thank God for them. Sometimes it's a spouse, a friend, a co-worker. Sometimes our salvation comes at the hand of a total stranger. Sometimes the *least of these* among us need to be saved (Matt 25). A hand up—or a hand out—so they can just make it through the day.[16] And sometimes, as we have learned this week, even the richest, the most well-educated, the most sophisticated, those who by every imaginable measure seem to be beyond need… sometimes even they need a bailout package.[17]

You and I need to be saved. If it is true in the hardscrabble of our everyday life, this truth is at least as true in a spiritual realm.[18] An incarnational theology of atonement teaches not that God sent Jesus to be a sacrifice, that God demanded a pound of flesh,[19] be it ours or his, but that if, as we claim, we have seen God in Jesus, it is God who dies. God for us. God with us. The cross always has been a scandal—because it shows that the only power God really has is the power to give life away. Yes, you and I need to be saved. And this salvation sometimes comes…at the price of blood.

So I think John Ballenger is right: We've got to find a way to leave the blood in.

May it be so!

Notes

[1] Baillie, Donald Macpherson, from his book, *God Was in Christ*, 1948, as quoted in *The Living Pulpit*, April-June 2007, Vol.16 No.2, p. 48. *The Living Pulpit* (eISSN 1946-1771) is published quarterly by The Living Pulpit, Inc., 475 Riverside Drive Suite 500, New York, NY 10115, USA.

[2] Robert Lowry, "Nothing but the Blood," 1876.

[3] William Cowper, "There Is a Fountain," 1771.

[4] Lewis E. Jones, "There is Power in the Blood," 1899.

[5] Andrae Crouch, "The Blood Will Never Lose It's Power," 1962.

[6] As a critique of such simplistic readings, Gail R. O'Day says, "The very richness of the text complicates the task of the interpreter. There is a temptation to pare down John 3:1–21 to its 'basic' elements—that is, either to summarize its story line (a Jewish religious authority comes to question Jesus) or its lesson (Jesus teaches about faith and judgment). Such summaries are easier to handle than the intricate dialogue and discourse of the text.... The interpreter needs to resist the temptation to distill this text to its essence or paraphrase its substance, however, because to do so does violence to [John's] way of storytelling and risks losing the text's proclamation of the good news." [O'Day, Gail R., *The New Interpreter's Bible Commentary, Vol. IX,* "John," (Nashville, TN: Abingdon Press), 503-504.] And for a more thorough discussion of biblical interpretation, and an alternative to a literal-only reading, see chapter two: "A New Question: Looking for the Spirit of the Message."

[7] Mark Heim, *The Christian Century* (March 14, 2001), 21.

[8] Quoted by Ted Schroder in a post titled, What Is the Main Point or Unique Element of Christianity?, July 17, 2015. (http://www.tedschroder.com/what-is-the-main-point-or-unique-element-of-christianity/). You can read the *The Mediator* by Emil Brunner at https://www.forgottenbooks.com/en/books/TheMediator_10119283

[9] Baillie, *God Was in Christ*, 48.

[10] I first learned this point with clarity in Leslie Weatherhead's book *The Will of God.* Weatherhead says unapologetically that God did *not* send Jesus to the earth to die—but so we might learn from his powerful life and his teachings. It was not by God's intent that Jesus was killed. Oppressive power and bad religion did that. In Weatherhead's language, Jesus's death was not the "intentional will" of God, but in the "ultimate will" of God, even an unforeseen, agonizing death can be used for good.

[11] This point is expanded in chapter 6 ("God Always Does Everything God Can Do") and in my upcoming book *The Power of the God Who Can't*, which expounds this theological affirmation in detail.

[12] I am indebted to Marcus Borg for this illustration. Jesus's death was sacrificial in the same way a firefighter's death can be called sacrificial. If the firefighter dies in the call of duty while saving a little girl from the flames, that death is a sacrifice, but because fire chiefs do not demand the death of their subordinates, such a death could not be called a substitution. The girl lived not because of the chief's demand, but because the fighter was willing to give his life in the course of his duty.

[13] From the prayer of St. Francis of Assisi.

[14] The May 2006 issue of *Christianity Today*, a theologically conservative publication, is titled, "No Substitute for the Substitute." The issue defends substitutionary atonement in light of the fact that a growing number of theologians in their own camp have expressed concern over this doctrine. The Green/Baker quotation is found on page 30.

[15] For the information from Mark Heim, see the September 5, 2006, issue of *The Christian Century*: "No more scapegoats: how Jesus put an end to sacrifice," 22ff.

[16] I weary of this distinction. Some people are so insistent that we need to give a "hand up not a handout." I understand, of course, that "if you give a man a fish you feed him for one day, but if you teach him to fish you feed him for a lifetime," but I suspect that much of our "concern" is really selfishly motivated. Sometimes people, ourselves included, need a handout, pure and simple. Let us be more willing to give—and to receive—such grace.

[17] The U.S. Congress this week passed the much belabored $700 billion bailout package for the U.S. economy.

[18] I recognize in my words here an ongoing argument I once conducted with my dear friend, the late Charlie Milford, who in his elder years espoused a "no atonement" theology. I don't know how widespread is this theology in Christian circles, but I have found it in the writing of Walter Wink of Auburn Theological Seminary. I do not have the exact citation before me, but there is a chapter in his book *Jesus and the Enigma of the Son of the Man* that deals with various atonement theologies. Charlie believed because we are created in the image of God, and because of God's unconditional love, that we do not need to be "saved." Salvation is "becoming in character who we (already are) in relationship." Though I agreed with much of Charlie's theological thought, and understand and appreciate much that led him to this conclusion, it is not one that I fully support. I still believe, in human terms—which perhaps give rise to our understanding of the theological affirmation—that we all have proven time and again our need for salvation.

[19] This phrase is originally attributed to Shylock in Shakespeare's *Merchant of Venice*: "The pound of flesh which I demand of him is deerely bought, 'tis mine, and I will haue it."

A New Way Home:
Believing It All…Differently

Questions to Consider

They talk about "falling in love." What is that? Is love really something beyond our control, something that "befalls" us?

Think of someone who has been married for fifty years. Did love just fall on them for five decades? What is the relationship between love and will and hard work?

People of faith say "God is love" and talk about "loving God." Is that something you just fall into? What does it really mean to "love God"?

What is the relationship of belief and faith? Do you have to believe to have faith? Do you have to have faith to believe?

The events of life "befall" us, but our response to these events is a matter of choice. How have you chosen to respond to the most dramatic events that have happened in your life?

What events stand out in your life as marking your journey? Make a brief outline here.

Faith is a "road to walk, not a place to stand." What steps will you choose to take today?

❖

I want to beg you, as much as I can, to be patient toward all that is unsolved in your heart and try to love the questions themselves like locked rooms and like books that are written in a very foreign tongue. Do not now seek the answers, which cannot be given you because you would not be able to live them. And the point is, to live everything. Live the questions now. Perhaps you will then gradually, without noticing it, live along some distant day into the answer.
—*Rainer Maria Rilke*[1]

I had an old friend who had spent fifty years in the church. He was a fine pastor with a distinctive ministry. He had been outspoken and personally active in a number of critical social issues of his day, and his ministry had been extremely influential to many people. Somewhere along the way, his path took a similar turn as mine has. The old dogmas failed to sustain. The questions became more important than the answers. The journey led him into unexpected territory.

On that journey his friends became influences, and the more he turned, the more everything began to look like more of the same—one turn just led to another; one rejection led to another more daring rejection. The path was exciting, the journey challenging and fulfilling. There were new vistas of exploration that deepened his views and understandings, but somewhere along the way, naming the place he had left seemed to become more important than claiming the steps he was taking. (And when you're always leaving a new place, finally there's not even any "home" to reject.) The questions had invited him into this bold exploration of faith, but someone has said it is difficult to celebrate a question, and this must have been true for my friend, who seemed less and less able to celebrate and more and more resolved that the way forward was by looking back. But rejecting what you do not believe rather than celebrating what you do believe is really not a way forward.

And what *did* he believe?

Or did he even *believe*?

Finally, sadly, honestly, he believed nothing. The last time I saw him, he was on his death bed, regretting the life he had wasted. They might have been the last words I heard him say: "It might have been all for nothing."

He had challenged me and had been an inspiration, a companion along my journey of questions, but maybe it was the hollow disappointment I saw in his dying eyes that spoke to me most loudly. Or maybe the loudest voice comes from the other end of the spectrum, the consistent texture of the faith my parents had planted in me so long ago. Maybe it is their consistent affirmation, rather than his disappointing rejection, that assures the sense of a "magnetic north" in my continued pursuit. The faith they planted in me is the faith they continue to make true with their lives, fulfilled and meaningful, lives endowed with a sense of intrinsic purpose, a connection to something deep and wide.

I will not die the death of disappointment. In the end, faith will not leave me filled with regret and emptied of hope. It will not happen.

I know this because even for a child of the church, faith only really begins with the undeniable leap everyone must take. Finally, it's not about intellect or rational deduction, but something more native. This doesn't mean faith is a primal, tribal reflex—it means faith is an instinct that is deep and deeply true. But then, after the initial leap, faith is like marriage: More important than the love that brings you together, if faith endures, it is the commitment that sustains. You leap into faith, and then you keep *deciding* with intellectual integrity; you keep *choosing* with courageous spirit; you keep *willing* with your whole heart…to believe.

It's not delusion. And it's not magic.

Faith takes work.

The path that led me far from home took a turn, unbeknownst to me. Where, when, how, I cannot say. Wisdom seldom asks our permission. As I continued along the way, however, unlike my friend who kept turning away until there was finally no longer a home to leave (so none to which he could return), my unorthodox path was quietly ushering me, even as I continued to move step by step away from home, back—into a deeper, richer faith. The path leading me away was, simultaneously, the light I needed to find my way back home.

As Kathleen Norris says, "It's been a lively journey. And I am the same person who departed, so long ago, and not the same at all."[2] With each step of critical reaction and rejection, a quiet voice of Wisdom was there, leading me with a refined understanding of affirmation and action to the faith that I never really ever departed. This paradoxical teacher allowed me to see in the childlike faith I was bequeathed not the superstitious words of antiquated religion, but ancient truth whose spiritual depths transcend the trappings and traditions of any age.

No, I will not die rejecting and, therefore, rejected. I will not allow the open palms with which I was so eager to receive to harden into angry fists of false pride that, bloody and beaten, finally give up and give over to an empty-handed faith. Instead, I will choose, day by day, to celebrate the journey that has led me so far from home, and I will thank God that the path will not lead me, ultimately, away from faith.

I am grateful for the way this path continues to afflict my comfort. Without it, I would not grow. Without it, I could not know. The pain and the growth go together. Eugene Peterson reflects on this irony in these words from his poem, "The Pain":

All pain's a prelude: to symphony, to sweetness.
"The pearl began as a pain in the oyster's stomach."[3]

I am equally grateful for the grace that has so often comforted the afflicted.[4] That affliction is inherent to doubt and dialogue. I have known the crisis that can come to the journey of faith ("Nothing is ever easy once you get educated!")—but I have never felt in danger of losing it, never been tempted to give it up, never burned with enough anger to denounce home, disavow trust, deny God.

That beautiful balance, the life-giving tension of challenge and affirmation that I have experienced, is not mine to claim with haughty arrogance. I know that many people of greater strength and deeper intellect have traveled my road and have chosen to go a different way. It is not my place to judge, nor my purpose, and I have no intent to preach a smug and self-assured autobiography—but I have chosen to remain faithful.

For all the people and experiences that have encouraged that choice, I am simply grateful.

Though I walk through the valley of the shadow…
I will not fear,
for thou art with me.

I have.
I did not.
Yes, I know.

I want only to celebrate the journey that has never let me go, but has, in the words of T. S. Eliot, brought me round so that I can know my home for the first time: "We shall never cease from exploration, and at the end of all exploring, we shall arrive at where we started but know that place for the first time."[5]

If my experience can shine light on the path you have traveled, I will be glad to have shared. If my words can be as a testimony to you, I will gladly preach. If my faith, feeble but steadfast, can serve as an example, I will be humbly honored.

When I die, with no look of disappointment in my eye, I want to claim without pride, but with deep confidence: "*I have fought the good fight, I have finished the race, I have kept the faith*" (2 Tim 4:7). I do not believe the life of ministry is based on delusion, nor does it traffic in deluding. I do not believe a heart devoted to God is out of touch with reality. I do not believe a mind content to ask every new question—and stay the course—has been deceived.

I do not believe a soul set on the never-ending horizon of tomorrow lives with false hope.

I simply believe the life of intentional, considered faith is the source of great strength.

It's not delusion. And it's not magic.

And the work of faith is worth all the effort.

Into my heart...

I could have rejected a devotional faith as shallow and sentimental. I chose instead to recognize that Albert Schweitzer's "longest journey," from the mind down to the heart, is also the truest quest. I am glad I have not lost heart and that the strong emotion I still feel does not empty my faith of its substance but only deepens my intellectual pursuit of it.

Once you get educated...

I could have become embittered by the questions. In anger, I could have rejected practice and belief, tradition and trial, grace and God. I am grateful for mentors who taught me that the only faith truly worth claiming is not the faith you've been given but the faith you have earned and learned.

Looking for the spirit of the message...

I could have let the contradictions in Scripture, the dated language, the antiquated settings cause me to regard all the words as hopelessly anchored to a dead past, with the baggage of centuries of misunderstanding and the bad theology that results. But for what literary treasure could that not be said? Words are always multilayered, concealing and revealing meanings like the layers of an onion. I am grateful to have learned to love the words—and then to peel away the surface, not throwing away the fruit before I began to plumb the depths.

Too many Christians aren't ready to live...

I could have decided that heaven was a silly notion, an idea created for the purpose of controlling weak people (give them a little pie in the sky, and we can put them through hell). I am grateful for a hope to which I can still cling, a hope based on love that never ends—never, ever ends—but a hope that gives as much meaning to our living as it could give to any next life.

A walk of joyful struggle...

I could have decided that the easy way was the only way, that joy comes in the morning only if there's no weeping the night before. I could have followed those who say church should always make you feel good, that the gospel is just a kind of comfort food for the soul. Instead, the questions came, and I will always be indebted to the mentors who were able to guide me through, teaching me to accept the questions and live with them. I am grateful to have learned that just like life, faith is a long and winding road.

Where you draw your lines...

I could have decided that there are no real truths, just arbitrary lines, random rules. I could have decided that relativism renders all wisdom meaningless. I'm grateful to have learned that there are lines, that definition is necessary (in material as well as spiritual things), and that boundaries are not the enemy. I'm glad I have learned to recognize the lines, even when they need to be crossed!

God always does everything Love can do...

I could have decided since God cannot do anything and everything I want God to do, there's no reason to believe, or (more foolishly) that there is no God in whom to believe. I hope I really have grown beyond that selfishness and into a deep appreciation of mystery and meaning and hope. I believe this is what "God" has always meant; the possibility that there is purpose is who God has always been.

Disciplined thinking...

I could have decided that blind faith is the only faith, that I needed only to "believe," that education is the enemy of the religious life. I'm grateful to have learned the truth spoken by Buckminster Fuller, that "faith is much better than belief. Belief is when someone else does the thinking."[6] The world of faith, opened by the world of critical thought, is multicolored and glorious. Though the world I once inhabited is an easier world, I would never go back to that world of black and white.

Everything that's true about Christianity...

I could have decided that all that matters are the facts I can measure and prove by empirical means. I'm glad I learned that the deepest truth has always been conveyed by the narratives that are more about my story than history. I'm grateful to have learned that the lessons of Scripture, the claims of faith, take a lifetime to live.

Leaving the blood in...

I could have decided that offensive words are always unredeemable. I could have learned to be critical and caustic, leading with cynicism and rejection, but my friends have taught me that the Truth is from the beginning. It is the word that God has been speaking from the very beginning. My mentors taught me that this word can be found in language, new and old, visual and auditory, that it can be studied and learned, but sometimes just sensed deep within. Truth is the rich wisdom at the core of philosophies and legends and dogmas, and it is ever richer when we have to dig to find it.

I could have wandered far from my home and lost my way. Instead, the little scraps of all the religion I thought I was leaving behind have turned out to be the crumbs of grace, markers leading me, surprisingly, joyfully, back home. It started in my home and in my heart, and I'm glad I can believe it all still—but so glad I've been taught to believe it all differently!

Thanks be to God.

Notes

[1] Rainer Maria Rilke, *Letters to a Young Poet,* (United States: Dover Publications, 2019).

[2] Kathleen Norris, *Amazing Grace: A Vocabulary of Faith,* (New York: Riverhead Books, 1999), 25.

[3] Peterson, Eugene, *The Contemplative Pastor: Returning to the Art of Spiritual Direction,* (Grand Rapids, MI: Eerdmans, 1993), 165.

[4] The quotation, as I learned it, referred to the gospel "to comfort the afflicted and to afflict the comfortable," but that is an adaptation of the original. A journalist named Finley Peter Dunne, writing for the *Chicago Evening Post,* introduced a fictional character into his humorous writing. "Mr. Dooley" was a fictional Irish bartender who became the mouthpiece for many of Dunne's opinions. The quotation originally appeared in a 1902 book titled, *Observations by Mr. Dooley:* "Th' newspaper does ivrything f'r us. It runs th' polis foorce an' th' banks, commands th' milishy, controls th' ligislachure, baptizes th' young, marries th' foolish, comforts th' afflicted, afflicts th' comfortable, buries th' dead an' roasts thim afterward."

[5] T S. Eliot, Anne Hodgson, and Philip Mairet, *Little Gidding,* (London: Faber and Faber, 1942), 59.

[6] "R. Buckminster Fuller Quotes." BrainyQuote.com. BrainyMedia Inc, 2020. 4 January 2020. https://www.brainyquote.com/quotes/r_buckminster_fuller_136967

About the Author

Russ Dean is a native of Blackstone, VA, but was raised in Clinton, SC. He is a graduate of Clinton High School ('82), Furman University ('86), the Southern Baptist Theological Seminary ('92), and he earned the Doctor of Ministry degree from the Beeson Divinity School of Samford University ('01).

He is married to his high school sweetheart, Amy Jacks Dean. After seminary, Amy and Russ served in different associate ministry positions on the staff of First Baptist Church, Clemson, SC, and then Russ became the Associate Pastor of Mountain Brook Baptist Church in Birmingham, AL. While in Birmingham, Amy served as the Associate Pastor of Riverchase Baptist Church. They came to Charlotte in October 2000 to become the Pastors of the Park Road Baptist Church, where they continue to share all pastoral responsibilities.

Russ is a regular, contributing editor for *Baptist News Global* and for *The Clinton Chronicle*, and he maintains a blog through his church's website, offering commentary on theological and current issues. In 2015 he was awarded the Richard Furman Baptist Heritage Award which recognizes a Furman graduate who reflects Baptist ideals by thinking critically, living compassionately and making life-changing commitments. Twice Russ has been invited to present a Christian perspective in the annual Comparative Religion Series sponsored by Charlotte's Temple Beth El. The 2013 topic was, "After Life… An End or a Beginning?" and the 2015 subject was "Science and Religion: Can They Coexist?" In 2015 Russ and Amy preached through the book of Mark, submitting the manuscript of those sermons for a biblical commentary series to be published by Smyth and Helyws Publishers.

Russ has been actively involved in ecumenical and interfaith work. He has served on the Governing Board of the North Carolina Council of Churches and served two terms, including two years as the president, of Mecklenburg Ministries. In 2013 he was recognized by Mecklenburg Ministries, sharing the Bridge-Builder Award with Dr. Rodney Sadler for their efforts in race relations. He currently serves as the President of the board of the Counseling Center at Charlotte and as Vice President of the board of the Educational Center. He has served as co-chair of the Racial and Economic Justice sub-committee of Charlotte's Clergy Coalition for Social Justice.

Russ and Amy have two boys, Jackson and Bennett, and their favorite past times involve watching their boys on a baseball field or a concert hall. When he is not with his sons or in the office Russ enjoys slalom and barefoot water skiing, woodworking, camping, and playing and writing music.

CPSIA information can be obtained
at www.ICGtesting.com
Printed in the USA
BVHW041708191221
624259BV00008B/17